One Man with Courage

One Man With Courage

✦

The Wayne Cryts Story

Jerry Hobbs

iUniverse, Inc.
New York Lincoln Shanghai

One Man With Courage
The Wayne Cryts Story

Copyright © 2005 by Jerry Hobbs

iUniverse books may be ordered through booksellers or by contacting:

iUniverse
2021 Pine Lake Road, Suite 100
Lincoln, NE 68512
www.iuniverse.com
1-800-Authors (1-800-288-4677)

ISBN-13: 978-0-595-37668-1 (pbk)
ISBN-13: 978-0-595-67541-8 (cloth)
ISBN-13: 978-0-595-82052-8 (ebk)
ISBN-10: 0-595-37668-1 (pbk)
ISBN-10: 0-595-67541-7 (cloth)
ISBN-10: 0-595-82052-2 (ebk)

Printed in the United States of America

Contents

Acknowledgements

I would like to thank Wayne and Sandy Cryts for letting us come in their home on numerous occasions to do the audio recording sessions and search through their artifacts. A special thank you goes to Sandy for the great chocolate chip cookies and milk that gave us the energy to put in those long hours and for having the faith in me to write this book.

I would also like to thank the following people for their contributions in getting this book ready to publish.

Don McRoy was our technical advisor, who among other things, audio taped Wayne telling his story, then transcribed it into written words for me to begin the writing process. He also scanned the pictures that were used in the book and researched various artifacts that were needed as well.

Loran Caldwell was a research assistant who went through all the journals and other artifacts gathering dates, names, and places that were needed for the book.

Alice Patrick, a retired English teacher from the Puxico School System, who proofread and edited the book.

Alden Nellis gave us permission to use some of the pictures that can be found in this book. He and his wife, Micki, published a documentary about the events that happened at the Ristine Elevator through the American Agriculture News back in 1981. Their website address is www.buffalo-creek-press.com.

Finally, I would like to thank my loving wife, Sharon, and my children that still live at home for their support while I spent many weekend and evening hours making this book a reality. I also have two older boys that didn't see me much during this time either. I love you guys very much!

Ristine Elevator Owners Bankrupt

Farmers have existed for thousands of years and go back to biblical times. The people of the world could not endure without us.

In 1896, William Jennings Bryan said, "Burn down your cities and leave our farms, and your cities will spring back up again as if by magic, but destroy our farms and the grass will grow in the streets of every city in the country."

Farming is unpredictable. It has its good days and its bad days and is very dependant on the climate that we live in. The weather directly affects our ability to make a living. We must overcome floods, droughts, erosion, and depleted soil conditions. But, we never imagined that we would have to fight the government too. And that is exactly what happened to me in 1981.

Most of the land that we farmed was east of New Madrid, Missouri, in the flood plains. The Mississippi River flooded out of its banks every year in this area, so we couldn't build grain storage bins there. In addition to that land, we had several farms rented around Puxico where we lived. But, it was just too costly to build storage bins on our farm in Puxico and transport the grain from New Madrid back up there. So, we rented space in the Ristine Elevator near New Madrid as we had done for years.

There were no limits on the length of time that we could store grain in the elevator as long as the storage fees were paid. So, we normally left our grain on deposit in the elevator until we thought the market price for grain had peaked, and then we would sell our grain and pay the storage fees. The James Brothers, Donald, George, and Robert of Corning, Arkansas, had purchased the Ristine Elevator in 1977. We deposited grain in the elevator with the new owners as we had done in the past with no problems.

In November and December of 1979, we deposited our grain in the elevator as usual, receiving warehouse receipts for verification of every bushel that we had stored there. Then, we took out a Commodity Credit Corporation (CCC) loan at the Agricultural Stabilization and Conservation Service (ASCS) office, using our soybeans as collateral since they were our private property. This was standard

1

procedure to enable us to pay our bills while the grain was in storage, and, like any other loan, we had to pay interest on the money that we borrowed. We could borrow $4.54 per bushel on the soybeans that we had on deposit in the elevator. At that time, we had 32,330 bushels of soybeans in the elevator and this allowed us to borrow $146,778. In December 1979, the market price for the grain was about $10.86 per bushel. If we would have sold our grain that day, we would have received $351,103.80.

This is where Wayne's grain was stored.

At harvest time, farmers had two options to choose from. The first option was to store the grain until the farmer decided the market price of the grain was at its peak, and the second option was to sell it at the time of delivery. In any year that we decided to choose the first option and deposited our grain in the Ristine Elevator, the owners of the elevator would charge us one twelfth of a cent per bushel per day.

With the first option, the elevator owners would issue us a warehouse receipt when we deposited our grain in the elevator. A warehouse receipt is a State Title showing that we owned the grain. Each warehouse receipt showed how many bushels of grain that we had stored in the elevator. The owners of the elevator were required to keep that grain in the elevator until we decided to sell it. When the decision was made to sell the grain, we would simply take the warehouse receipts to the elevator office and tell them we wanted to sell our grain. At that time, a check would be written to us for the grain at the current market price. Then, we would take the check to the bank, deposit it in our account, and go to the ASCS office to pay off the Commodity Credit Loan.

If we chose the second option and sold our grain as we unloaded it at the elevator, then a scale receipt would be given to us that listed the weight, foreign material, number of bushels, and the market price that we sold it for. Then, they would write us a check for the grain at that time.

In 1979, we had made the decision to store our grain in the Ristine Elevator because the price per bushel was still climbing. We were feeling very good about our future at that time.

Then, one afternoon while I was on the road attending an American Agriculture Movement (AAM) meeting, I called home to talk to my wife to see how she was doing.

Sandy said, "Wayne, we just heard on the news that the Ristine Elevator went bankrupt."

I was very concerned, because we had over $350,000 worth of grain stored there. So, I immediately turned around and came home. When I made it home, the first thing I did was call the Missouri Department of Agriculture in Jefferson City.

At that time, I was on Governor Teasdale's Agriculture Advisory Council and I knew most of the people that worked in the Missouri Department of Agriculture. I asked to speak to Tom Hopkins. When he got on the phone, I said, "Tom, this is Wayne, I heard that the Ristine Elevator went bankrupt."

He said, "Yes Wayne, the elevator went bankrupt, but don't become concerned. We have been monitoring the elevator, and when we got word that they were going to take grain out of the elevator and sell it without entering it on their records, we went in and padlocked the elevator. We have measured the grain and all the grain is there. It's going to take a period of two or three weeks to get the red tape out of the way, and then you farmers will be able to get your grain."

Tom's comments really relieved my mind. I thought, "This was going to be a simple process."

Then, a federal judge in Arkansas by the name of Charles Baker got involved, took jurisdiction, and declared it a federal bankruptcy case since the James Brothers owned elevators in Missouri and Arkansas. From the beginning, Judge Baker contended that since the grain was in the elevator at the time the owners went bankrupt, he was going to sell the grain free and clear of all liens to payoff the debts of the elevator owners.

The judge claimed that all the property, equipment, and grain were part of the elevator owners' assets, with an estimated value of $5 to $6 million. Judge Baker appointed Robert Lindsey as the trustee who would oversee the bankruptcy procedures. Robert Lindsey would receive a percentage of all the assets as payment for his services during the whole bankruptcy process.

I immediately started saying, "Hey, this is not right. The grain in the elevators is our private property and we have warehouse receipts to prove it. No one should have the right to sell our private property to pay off someone else's debts."

Imagine how you would feel if something similar had happened to you. Most people have used parking garages for one reason or another. Suppose you park your vehicle in a parking garage to go watch a ballgame. You pay your fee, get your receipt to rent a space in a parking garage and go park your vehicle. And then, while you were enjoying the ballgame, the owners of the parking garage declare bankruptcy. After the ballgame is over, you walk back to the parking garage, all excited that your team had won, and you discover that the parking garage is locked down. Some police officers tell you that the owner has filed bankruptcy and has reported everything in the building as his property and that your vehicle is going to be sold to help pay his debts. How many people would stand by and accept this? It would be Un-American to allow that to happen.

Well, that is what happened to me. I was paying storage fees on the beans and had made no contract to sell the beans to the elevator owners. I was merely renting space in the elevator until I decided to sell my crop. This was something that millions of farmers across the United States had done for years.

I had warehouse receipts for every bushel of soybeans that I had stored in the grain elevator. Warehouse receipts are considered proof of ownership for the grain, just like the title to a vehicle. Banks will loan money on them as well as the Commodity Credit Corporation (CCC). The warehouse receipts are used as collateral for the loan. Each warehouse receipt has the following statement written on it: "Upon return of this receipt, properly endorsed, and payment of the warehouseman's lien claimed hereon (Storage Fees), said grain of the same or better grade will be delivered to the above named depositor on his order."

The federal judge in Little Rock, Arkansas, had usurped the power of the State of Missouri that was responsible for licensing, bonding, and auditing the grain storage warehouses. Missouri's Grain Warehouse Law gives the Missouri Department of Agriculture the power to ensure that grain stored in Missouri warehouses are maintained 100% by quantity and grade and that it is not shipped or sold without the farmer's consent.

When Judge Baker took this step, the State of Missouri began to fight for jurisdiction over the elevators in an effort to make a determination of ownership of the grain and get it back to the farmers. The State of Missouri felt like they should have jurisdiction over the elevators in Missouri, because it had Police and Regulatory Authority.

While this process was going on, a farmer from Piggott, Arkansas, called me concerning a storage elevator that the James Brothers owned down there, which was part of the bankruptcy proceedings. He asked me if grain was being hauled out of the elevator in Missouri so that it could be sold to pay the debts of the James Brothers. I told him that we were monitoring it closely and that the grain was still in the elevator, because the Missouri Department of Agriculture had locked down the elevator.

The Arkansas farmer said, "Wayne, they have started hauling grain out of the elevators down here." He asked me to come down and talk to them.

The very next day, I went down to Piggott. I told the farmers about the phone call that I received from a farmer in Nebraska. That farmer said, "If you let them haul the grain out of there, it's gone, and you won't get but a few pennies on the dollar for the grain that you own."

The Arkansas farmers, however, didn't do anything to stop them. They just stood by and watched them haul all their grain out of the elevators.

Because of the jurisdictional fight between the State of Missouri and the federal judge in Arkansas, the farmers in Missouri were concerned about what was going to happen here. We were watching that situation very closely and hoping our state government would win jurisdiction over the elevators since we knew our state officials would do what was right.

A few days later, while I was setting in my home watching the six o'clock news, KFVS 12 reported that the Ristine Elevator was going to open for business as usual the next morning at ten o'clock. I immediately called N.J. Nowell at New Madrid, because he had the second largest amount of grain deposited at the Ristine Elevator, with around 21,000 bushels. When he answered the phone, I said, "N.J., this is Wayne. Did you see the report on the news about opening the Ristine Elevator for business tomorrow?"

He said, "Yes, in fact I was getting ready to call you."

I said, "N.J., I don't know about you, but I don't want them opening up that elevator unless we are going to get our grain. And I don't think we should let them haul our grain out of it until we get a ruling from the State of Missouri letting us know what's going on."

When N.J. agreed, I told N.J. that I had a tractor and disk on the Marcy Farm by Kewanee and that I was going to take it over to the scales at the elevator and block it so no grain could be removed.

He said, "That sounds good to me. In fact, I have a tractor and disk on a farm just a little ways up from there. We will get it and meet you at the elevator tomorrow."

The next morning, Sandy and I went over to the Marcy farm, and I got on the tractor and headed to the elevator. As I was going by N.J. Nowell's farm, he was just getting his tractor started and pulled out behind me. When we got there, I pulled in on the scales and unfolded the disk on my tractor. Then, N.J. pulled around behind me on his tractor and unfolded his disk. This was the beginning of the blockade of the Ristine Elevator.

By this time, it was the later part of August 1980. We normally would have had our grain sold from the previous year by March or April at the latest, but this year was different. The price of grain was still going up and we decided that we would be O.K., if we could get our grain out soon.

We had already planted our 1980 crop and we were having the worst drought that we had seen in many years. The crop that we had planted that year was burning up and we knew that it would not yield much grain at harvest time. However, we were thinking that if we lost the crop in the field due to drought, then we would still be O.K. by selling the grain that we had deposited in the elevator at twice what we would normally get for it.

So, here we are in an economic dilemma: one of our crops burning up in the field and the one that we wanted to sell was tied up in bankruptcy court. We knew we couldn't overcome the loss of two crops in two consecutive years. We were looking at our whole family farming operation going down the tubes. It was becoming an economic necessity to get our grain out of the elevator and get it sold. We needed to pay off our CCC loan and storage fees, as well as other debts related to our farming needs. That put more pressure on us than we would have normally been under. When we went in with the tractors and blocked the scales at the elevator, we felt like that was the only hope we had to protect the grain we had deposited in the elevator and keep it there until the courts could determine ownership.

When Judge Baker found out that we used our tractors to blockade the elevator, he sent in federal marshals to take full custody of the property, protect the elevator, and the assets in it. Then, they were supposed to open up the elevator to farmers that had fall delivery contracts with the elevator owners.

These fall delivery contracts had been made earlier in the year. A farmer could make a contract for the grain at a pre-determined price per bushel while the crop was still growing in the field. When the crop was harvested in the fall and delivered to the elevator, the contract would be paid off at the previously agreed upon price. When the farmer did this, he was taking a gamble that the contracted price was higher than it would be at harvest time. After the dollar amount was set and the contract was signed, that amount was what the farmer got for his grain, no matter when it was deposited in the elevator. I have seen some farmers do very well by contracting their grain before it was harvested at say $8.00 per bushel and delivering it at a time when the price had dropped to $5.00 per bushel. On the other hand, I have seen just the opposite happen, too.

Federal Marshals Arrive

When the federal marshals arrived at the elevator on September 16, 1980, they told us they were not going to allow any grain to be hauled out of the elevator, but they were going to open it up for those farmers that had contracted fall delivery on their grain.

Of course, we knew that no farmer wanted to haul his grain to an elevator that had filed bankruptcy. A person would be silly to do that when he knew he would not be paid for it.

So, we told the marshals that we had no problem letting any farmers come in and deposit their grain in the elevator. The marshals said, "You mean you would be willing to move your tractors off of the scales?"

Agreeing we said, "Sure, as long as the trucks are bringing grain in and not taking it out of the elevator."

They said, "All right, fair enough."

That was the first agreement we made with the federal marshals. At that point, we moved the tractors off the scales and setup camp there.

However, none of the farmers delivered their grain to the elevator since the owners had filed bankruptcy. Those farmers did not want to bring their grain to the elevator for two reasons. First, they knew that they would not be paid for their grain since the judge had declared that the grain would be sold free and clear of all liens with the money being put in an escrow account. Second and more importantly, the price of beans was continuing to climb all summer and throughout the fall. They knew that they could get much more money for their grain by selling it through a solvent elevator. And I'm sure their lawyers probably contended to the trustee that these farmers could not bring their grain to the Ristine Elevator since there was no telling what those crazy farmers that had blockaded the scales might do.

When the bankruptcy trustee realized that none of those farmers were going to haul in their grain, the trustee sued those twenty farmers that had not delivered their contracted grain for the face value of contract. The bankruptcy trustee insisted that the court force the farmers to put their grain in the elevator, because

8

he got a percentage of all the assets of the elevator as payment for his services during the bankruptcy.

Wayne's Dad and Mom visit with him at the Ristine Elevator office.

I'm not sure exactly what the outcome was with those twenty farmers, but I hope the judge dropped the suit against them. And I hope they were able to sell their grain for a profit to meet their financial obligations. However, the one thing that I am sure of was that those farmers never brought any of their grain to the Ristine Elevator.

Well, when the federal marshals told us they were going to be sleeping in the office of the grain elevator, we decided to set up camp there also. We brought our cots in and slept right there with them. We had someone there along with the federal marshals twenty-four hours a day, watching the whole process. We got well acquainted with the federal marshals during this time. Their names were Bob Bailey and George Welch. Once we got to know them, we found them to be honest and fair, but stern.

I will never forget one Sunday afternoon at the elevator. We were having a big picnic outside and enjoying each other's company. About midway through the meal, I decided to go check on the marshals and find out if they wanted something to eat. When I walked into the office, I saw a bunch of little ol' kids in there. The federal marshals were babysitting our kids while the rest of us were out enjoying the picnic. That's the kind of guys they were.

I can't say enough about the professionalism of the federal marshals. They had their job to do, but they literally got caught up in this thing. They discovered that the farmers were nice, decent, hard working people who were in the middle of an unfortunate mess. We sat around talking with the federal marshals about our dilemma. And once the federal marshals realized the situation that we were in, I think they really sympathized with us.

I was in the elevator office one morning when the phone rang and Bob Bailey answered it. I could only hear his side of the conversation.

He kept saying, "Sir, you don't understand. Sir, you don't understand." Finally, he said, "Sir, if you can do this job better that I can; you come down here, get my badge, and you arrest him yourself, because I'm not going to."

When Bob got off the phone, he turned around and said, "How in the world do they expect us to arrest a bunch of farmers and their families when they are right?"

The next day Larry Strahorn, Head of the Federal Marshals Office in St. Louis, had come to the elevator. He had come to the elevator office to see what was going on himself. I assume that he was the person that Bob had been talking to on the phone the day before. Marshal Strahorn had a hard-nosed attitude and he meant business. I'm sure he thought he could come in there and take care of that situation in a short matter of time.

He told us that the farmers were going to have to leave the facilities. I told him to look around. There is over twenty-three acres of unfenced land around here and there was no way he could keep us out. Then, Marshal Strahorn told us that he wanted to go out to the bins and look inside them. Well, that meant that the federal marshals, Missouri State Agriculture officials, and the farmers had to take their locks off of the doors. When we finally got all that done, the Marshal was able to see what all the commotion was about. However, the longer he stayed there and the better he got to know us, the more he got caught up in the farmers' dilemma as well.

During this time, there were bankruptcy hearings being held at various sites in Arkansas and Missouri. Officials from the State of Missouri were attending the hearings in Arkansas as well and since I was on Governor Teasdale's Agriculture Advisory Council, I was allowed to go with them. The state officials would drive to most of the hearings in Missouri, but they flew to the hearings that were held in Arkansas. They would land at Dexter, pick me up, and off we would go again.

As I attended these hearings, I began to notice that every time the James Brothers and their wives would walk into the courtroom, they would shake hands and laugh with the trustee who was appointed by the judge. They also acted like he and the other lawyers that were there working on the case were their best friends. I also noticed that their wives had on lots of expensive jewelry and clothing, while we farmers and Missouri State officials were made to feel like second-class citizens.

We were attending a hearing in Kennett, Missouri, and I happened to see Mr. Stillman, an attorney from Kennett who was there working on a different case. I knew him and asked if he would talk to Judge Baker to find out if he would meet with me. I honestly did not think the judge knew all the facts about what was going on and what kind of situation the farmers were in.

Mr. Stillman said, "Wayne, I think the judge would probably like to talk to you."

Mr. Stillman went in the judge's chambers to ask if he would be willing to talk to me. He came back out after only being in there a few minutes. I asked him what the judge had said. Mr. Stillman told me and other farmers standing there that the judge said, "I don't want to talk to Wayne Cryts or any of those damn farmers." I was shocked to hear that a federal judge would respond that way.

The next day, I announced that we were going to the elevator to remove our grain. We did not really intend to do so, but we wanted to keep the courts moving toward making a determination of ownership of the grain. Upon hearing this information, the federal marshals requested that the Governor send in Missouri State Troopers to help protect them and maintain control of the elevator. The next morning, several of us met across the road from the elevator to organize. We talked for some time about what we were going to do and decided to march in.

We crossed the road on foot, carrying the American flag, the Missouri flag, and the Christian flag. My brother was behind us in one of our grain trucks. As we approached the elevator, several federal marshals and state troopers were there waiting on us. We continued walking toward them. The federal marshals were in front and the state troopers had two cars blocking the entrance behind them. We just marched right through them between the cars. They stood there and didn't do anything. My brother kept coming with the truck, but when he reached the state troopers' cars, he stopped. Later, he told me that if I had looked back and motioned him through, he would have kept on going. But I didn't, and I'm glad I didn't. We did not want any violence. We had accomplished our goal of putting pressure on the federal judge and the State of Missouri to continue moving this process along.

Governor Teasdale sent Jack Runyan, Secretary of Agriculture of the State of Missouri, down the next day to try to help negotiate the situation. The Governor had decided that he wanted the state troopers out of there, because he did not want them going against the farmers. As long as the state troopers were there, the Governor was directly involved. This was quickly becoming a hot political issue and Governor Teasdale did not want to get caught in the middle of it.

The farmers wanted the State of Missouri to keep fighting for state's rights. We knew that if the State of Missouri could get jurisdiction, we would be in good shape and would be able to get our grain back. We also knew it might take a while, but we wanted them to stay in this battle and fight for us.

When Director Runyan arrived, he met with some of the farmers in front of the elevator while I was inside talking to Federal Marshals, Bob Bailey and George Welch. During this time, one of my friends, J.D. Gott, had driven a truck that had a half of a load of milo in it to the back side of the elevator and up on the scales. Then, J.D. dumped that load of grain on the scales.

This alarmed Jack Runyan and he came running in the office and said, "Wayne, they have done it now! They have dumped grain on the scales and now the federal marshals are not going to let the state troopers leave!"

He was afraid we were going to be arrested, so we all rushed outside to see what he was talking about. Things got very exciting around there for a little while.

I'll never forget that incident. The federal marshals, state troopers, and we farmers were all standing out there talking about the grain that had just been dumped on the scales. Then, George Foster from Puxico walked up and started talking with us about that too. Suddenly, we heard this noise that sounded like a gun going off. One of the state troopers grabbed for his gun, and George grabbed his hand. They just stood there staring at each other for a minute, and we could feel the tension in the air. Then, someone started laughing, which caused the rest of us to begin laughing. That was just what we needed to get the situation under control. The marshals and I looked at each other and said, "We're alright, we're alright." Later, we found out that someone had thrown a rock up against the tin on the grain bin. Several things like that happened during the months we shared possession of the elevator.

Shortly after this incident, we were told that Governor Teasdale and the Missouri Department of Agriculture had obtained a temporary injunction in the Missouri Circuit Court of New Madrid County that allowed the Missouri Director of Agriculture, Jack Runyon, "to take possession of and seize by physical means, if required, the grain warehouses that the James Brothers owned in Missouri along with the grain and records contained therein."

When Judge Baker received the temporary injunction giving Director Runyon authority to take possession of the elevators, he filed contempt of court charges against him and the Governor. A federal appeals court heard the case and Judge Howard ordered Judge Baker to produce good and valid reasons for filing the contempt of court charges. Judge Baker refused to honor Judge Howard's jurisdiction and would not do so. At that point, Governor Teasdale, Director Runyan, and the State of Missouri fell out of the fight. They just threw up their hands and left us farmers there to fight the federal authorities on our own.

I believe in my own heart that if Governor Teasdale would have stayed in the battle and would have been willing to go to jail for the farmers, he would have been elected to a second term as Governor of the State of Missouri with a bright political future ahead of him. But that was not to be. Now, we were on our own to continue the fight to protect our private property.

The situation continued to worsen. One Saturday morning, a train with five hopper cars was sent in to load the grain that was in the Ristine Elevator. When the train stopped, we met with the officials on the train and told them that we thought it would be better if they took the train back where it came from. They did not want any trouble, so they got back on the train and left. We were determined to keep the grain in the elevator until a determination of ownership could be made by the judge. We knew that if we ever let them load the grain and sell it, we would see very little of that money.

Tremendous Financial Strain

In the mean time, my family had harvested what little crops we could that fall because of the drought and began marketing the grain. But, the harvest was so poor that we could not make enough money off of it to pay our bills. By that time, we had two years worth of bills piling up on us and we were forced to refinance our loans at a higher rate of interest. This put us into a real financial bind. I decided that if we were going to have a chance to save the family farm, I had to get my grain out of the elevator. I seemed to have no other option since Judge Baker was determined to sell our grain free and clear of all liens and we were not making any progress toward a determination of ownership of the grain.

Then, I had a glimmer of hope that the dispute over the ownership of the grain could be resolved legally, was rekindled from another source.

One evening, a farmer from Minnesota called and said, "Wayne, I think we have a solution to your problem. Do all the farmers at the Ristine Elevator have Commodity Credit Loans?"

I said, "Yes, they all have Commodity Credit Loans."

He said, "Our elevator went bankrupt up here a few years ago and we asked our congressman to talk to the CCC about buying our equity in the grain. We asked them to assume our CCC loans and pay us the difference between the loan and the market price of the grain and they agreed. In doing so, they became the sole owner of the grain. This took the farmers out of the middle of the bankruptcy procedures and that solved our problem."

I thanked him for the call and thought to myself, "This was the answer to our prayers."

I immediately called our Congressman, Bill Burleson, and told him what the farmer in Minnesota told me. Then, I asked him to set up a meeting with the United States Department of Agriculture in Washington, D.C. He said that would be fine and set up an appointment for us to meet with them. When we got there, I was introduced to the Under Secretary for Farm and Foreign Agriculture Services. I explained to him what I had been told by the farmer in Minnesota. I told him that the CCC had assumed their loans and paid those farmers the difference between the CCC loan and the market price of the grain to get them out of the bankruptcy procedures. Then, the CCC took over as sole owner of the grain. The Under Secretary liked that idea and agreed to the proposal.

But, Arnold Grundelman, an attorney with the Department of Agriculture, was setting there listening to our conversation. Mr. Grundelman said, "No, we cannot agree to that. It's against legal counsel's advice."

The Under Secretary said, "What do you mean against legal counsel's advice? There is a precedence that has already been established for this. It's been done before."

Arnold said, "Yes, but it's against my advice. In fact, we consider ourselves adversaries with the farmers in this case."

This was the first time I had ever seen Congressman Burleson get that mad. He grabbed the table and it shook as he stood up, and he said, "What do you mean, we are adversaries with the farmers? This is the United States Department of Agriculture! We are not adversaries with the farmers!"

When the meeting was over, I was still hopeful that we had found a solution to our problem. However, later on that week, I was given notification that the USDA would not get involved if legal counsel advised against it. Since Arnold Grundelman had advised them not to get involved, that ended our hopes of getting help from the United States Department of Agriculture.

A short time later, after I had returned home to Puxico, a farmer from Oklahoma called to tell me about his experience with an elevator owner that had filed bankruptcy there. I don't remember his name, but I could tell that he was an older gentleman and I could hear the pain in his voice as he spoke.

He said, "Wayne, we went through the same thing here in 1976 that you are going through there. Our elevator went bankrupt and we lost everything because of it. I just want you to think about something. At this point, you don't have anything to lose because you have already lost it. But you have a chance to get it back as long as the grain is in that elevator. However, if you allow them to sell the grain, money from the sale will be put in an escrow account in a bank somewhere and you ain't going to go rob a bank."

He explained to me that the judge in Oklahoma had ordered all the grain in the elevator to be sold and the proceeds from the sale of the grain was to be put in an escrow account until ownership of the grain could be determined. Once that money was put into an escrow account, it was just like an ice cube. It started to melt away as the judge started deducting the trustee fees, attorney's fees, payroll taxes, and all the expenses associated with it.

He said, "Wayne, they will milk it dry. The court case will drag on for three or four years and by the time they make a determination that it's your grain, there won't be anything left."

I thought about what that gentleman had said for a while and realized that that was exactly what Judge Baker plans to do in this case. Then, I told my family what the farmer from Oklahoma had said, and we talked about that for a few days. After much thought and consideration, that man's words became our guiding light when the decision was made to remove our grain from the elevator. I knew that we didn't have anything to lose. If we stood by and watched them remove our grain, it would be gone forever. But, at this point, we still had a chance to get it back and that was the only hope I had of saving our five generation family farm.

In the mean time, Judge Baker had set a date for a hearing to determine ownership of the grain. It was to be held at the Federal Court House in Little Rock, Arkansas. I hired a lawyer out of Cape Girardeau, Missouri, by the name of Dick Jones with Oliver, Oliver, and Jones to represent me. When my family received notification from the court that a hearing date had been set by the judge, we met our lawyer and drove down to Little Rock. I had to pay my lawyer by the hour from the time we left home until we returned. Since we always drove down the day before, the hours added up quickly. I also had to rent the motel rooms and pay for all the meals.

The hearing was scheduled to begin at 10:00 a.m. When we walked into the courtroom, we were told that the hearing had been postponed. We asked why we were not notified prior to coming down to Little Rock. But, we were not given a reason. The court officials just told us that we would be notified later when a new court date would be set. So, we got back in the car and drove home. I had paid the lawyer, rented rooms, and bought meals for nothing.

Two weeks later, I was notified that a new court date had been set. This time, I decided that I would call the court clerk the day before we were scheduled to be there to verify that the hearing had not been postponed. I made the call, asked to speak to the clerk, and he confirmed that the hearing was still set for 10:00 a.m. My lawyer and I drove to Little Rock and rented a room for the night. The next morning, we walked into the courtroom only to find out that the hearing was postponed again. This was very frustrating and expensive, and it happened several times as the case continued. I believe Judge Baker was doing this not only to drag out the proceedings in the hopes that we would give up, but also to get more money for the trustee and bankruptcy lawyers.

At times when we actually had a hearing, there would not be much discussion about the ownership of the grain. The judge would ask the lawyers and trustee to submit their bills. The bailiff would take the judge their bills and he wouldn't even look at them. He just approved them, hit the gavel on the bench, and dismissed court.

This process went on for months. Finally, the judge set a hearing in which my lawyer was able to present a very convincing case with documentation of the warehouse receipts and facts proving my ownership of the grain. With these facts and documentation, making a judgment in my favor should have been a very simple process. But, Judge Baker had already started making his ruling before my lawyer could sit down after making his final summation of the facts. The judge did not dismiss himself to review the facts or think about anything. He just denied my claim of ownership and walked out.

When I looked around the courtroom that day, I saw the trustee, six bankruptcy lawyers, and Arnold Grundelman, the lawyer that I met in Washington, D.C., at the USDA office. After the judge made his ruling against me, they all turned to look at me and grinned. I really felt like this was a systematic denial of justice, so they could make a profit from us. At that moment in time, I remembered the phone call from the farmer in Oklahoma who told me that the longer a bankruptcy case dragged on, the more money the trustee, lawyers, and possibly the judge, made.

After I came back from that hearing, I sat down with my wife Sandy and my children, Terry and Paula, to discuss what we should do. We finally decided that it was time to go get our grain.

I said, "If we do this, we have to be willing to follow it through to the end, no matter what happens."

My ancestors had been involved in farming for five generations, and we all agreed that this was the only option we had left to possibly save the family farm.

Then, we began to think about what could happen to us if we did this. We could be injured, go to jail, or even be killed attempting to remove our grain. We could lose everything we had if anything went wrong. We asked our selves again, "Are we willing to take that risk?" Once again, it was a unanimous decision. We had decided to go to the Ristine Elevator and remove our private property.

We also knew that we might be there by ourselves, and we wondered if we could fight this battle alone, without the support from our friends and other farmers in the area. Finally, we decided that we had no other choice but to go through with it. We were committed to do our very best to go as far as we could, no matter what happened. It is hard to imagine a family sitting around a table having to make such a hard decision as that, knowing we could lose everything that we had worked so hard to build.

After the decision was made, I went to the elevator and told everybody there that we had made the decision to get our grain. They started asking me a lot of questions about when and how we were going to do that. I told them that I didn't have any details at that time because we had just made the decision; however, I would meet with them again when I had a plan in place.

I decided to go talk to Bill Anderson, better known as Cousin Carl, who worked at the radio station, KSIM, in Sikeston, Missouri. Bill had been covering this story from the beginning and we had become well acquainted during this time. Through our conversation, I began to develop a plan to get my grain back.

I said, "Bill, my family and I have decided that we are going to the elevator to remove my grain."

"Wayne, are you serious about that? Is that your decision or are you being influenced by someone else?" Bill asked.

"Bill, it was a family decision. We're going to do it."

"When are you planning to do this?"

"Well, I think I can get everything ready to go by Monday."

At this point, Bill said, "Wayne, let me give you some advice. While I have been covering this story, I have discovered that you not only want to get your grain out of the elevator, but you believe this law should be changed. Is it an unjust law?"

I said, "Yes Bill, I really believe it is."

Then, he said, "You probably don't have any idea how much national attention this is gaining do you?"

When I told him that I did not, he said, "This thing is going nation-wide. If you are really going to do this, I think you should have a press conference and announce what you are going to do. You have been open and honest with everyone so far and I know that you have talked to everybody from the local authorities to the state and federal officials about your problem. I really believe you should hold a press conference."

After I told Bill that I didn't know how to set up a press conference, he told me, "There's nothing to it. I'll just put it out on the wire service and notify the media that you are going to hold a press conference to announce that you are planning to remove your grain from the Ristine Elevator, and we will go from there."

I told him that would be fine. Bill asked me when I wanted to have the press conference and I told him that we might as well do it tomorrow.

He laughed again and said, "We will need a little more time than that."

So, we set the press conference for January 15, 1981, which gave us about a week to make our plans. Then, we started talking about how I needed to handle the press conference and what I should say. Then, Bill told me that I would need to announce the facts: first, that I was going in to remove my grain and second, the date and time that it would happen.

My first thought was to remove the grain the next day after the press conference while the press was still here. Then I said, "Bill, let me look at the calendar."

Bill handed me the calendar and while I was looking at it, I just happened to flip it over to the next month and saw February 16, George Washington's Birthday.

I thought, "How appropriate. I believe that President Washington would roll over in his grave if he knew that the United States Department of Agriculture considered themselves as adversaries with the American farmer."

I said, "Bill, I'm going to do it February 16 at ten o'clock in the morning. George Washington and this country's founding fathers took a stand against the King of England over laws they believed to be unjust."

He said, "All right, let's do it."

I had no idea at that time how important that decision was. If I had decided to remove the grain the day after the press conference, the media would not have had enough time to report the news across the nation. By setting the date to remove the grain a month after the press conference, we gave people time to hear about our dilemma and to make plans to come and help us. Surprisingly, people came from all over the country to help us. These people were not just farmers, but were from a wide range of occupations.

We made all the arrangements for the press conference that day and decided to hold it at the Ramada Inn in Sikeston, Missouri, on January 15. On the day of the press conference, I announced, "If it has not been determined that this grain is my private property by February 16, then I will go to the Ristine Elevator at 10:00 a.m. and remove it."

I told everyone that the state officials and congressmen had been sympathetic about the situation, but were unwilling to go against a federal judge. I said, "We feel that what they are doing to us is a gross miscarriage of justice, and my family and I are willing to go to jail if necessary."

I also informed them that every farmer who had a warehouse receipt could come with us and we would help them load their trucks as well. Finally, I told them that I was not a radical farmer, and I did not want anybody bringing any type of firearm or become violent in any way.

That message went across the country like wildfire. Within a day or two, we had people calling to let us know that they were going to come and help us. Many of them told us they had had similar experiences and they ended up losing everything and wished that they had been brave enough to do the same thing. A few people were talking pretty rough and were planning to use violence if necessary. I told all the people that called that I really appreciated their support, but if they were planning to bring guns and use violence, then please stay home. We will not have any of that, because we did not want anybody to get hurt.

During this time, the American Agriculture Movement (AAM) was having a convention in Pueblo, Colorado. I was a member and was invited to go out there and speak to them. Sandy and I decided to take a charter bus out there and about forty people from this area rode the bus with us.

When it was my turn to speak at the convention, I told them about our struggles and what had happened to us. I also informed them of every effort that I had made to talk to the authorities in the courts and to the local, state, and federal government to get this issue resolved. I also told them that I planned to work hard to get the federal bankruptcy law changed so that no one else had to suffer great financial loses. Finally, I explained to the people that I truly believed that I had no other choice, but to remove my grain from the Ristine Elevator.

Afterwards, numerous people came up to me and said they were going to be there to support me. When we got home, the reality of this whole thing was beginning to set in. You can't possibly imagine how much pressure we were under as we went through this. This pressure continued to grow the closer it got to February 16.

One evening as February 16 was drawing nearer, I was at home when Robert Lindsey, the trustee for the Ristine Elevator bankruptcy case, called me. Our conversation brought a little light of hope again to the situation, maybe I wouldn't have to take drastic measures to get my grain back.

Mr. Lindsey said, "Wayne, I would like to meet with you to see if we can't get this problem resolved."

"Mr. Lindsey, I would be glad to meet with anybody that could help get this thing resolved and behind us."

"I really don't feel comfortable going to Missouri. Would you be willing to come to Arkansas?" Mr. Lindsey asked.

"Sure, I don't have a problem with that."

"Would you care to meet me at the Holiday Inn at Jonesboro? We will have lunch and see if we can come to an agreement."

So, we set a date and time to meet at the Holiday Inn. Sandy and I drove down and met with Mr. Lindsey. We had dinner together and when we finished he said, "Wayne, we want to get this thing resolved and you know you are the one that's causing us problems. If you will stop the fight that you are carrying on with us, I will assure you that you will receive all of your grain, or money equivalent to it, if you will just 'drop it'."

I said, "That's fine. All I want is my grain. How about the other farmers that have grain in the elevator? Will they get their grain?"

Mr. Lindsey said, "No. This deal is just between us. The other farmers are not going to be apart of this deal."

I said, "Mr. Lindsey, I don't feel comfortable making a deal where I get all of my grain and the rest of the farmers don't. I just can not accept that."

He said, "Wayne, you are going to get everything that's yours."

I told him that I appreciate that, but I would also like to see all the other farmers get everything that was theirs too. We went back and forth for quite sometime. Then, he got upset that I wouldn't negotiate a deal with him.

Finally, he said, "I think we should end this meeting, since we are at an impasse."

I said, "Mr. Lindsey, I just don't understand why you are willing to let me have my grain and the other farmers can't have theirs. It's their grain. It doesn't belong to anybody else."

He hardly had anything else to say after that. The meeting broke up, we shook hands, and went our separate ways. The light of hope was again extinguished.

Not long after that meeting, the President of the First Tennessee Bank called. He introduced himself and asked if I would be willing to meet with him and some of the First Tennessee Bank officials in Memphis to try to resolve this problem, because the bank had a large stake in the elevator bankruptcy.

I said, "Sure, I would be happy to meet with you," hoping again that the problem could be solved without being forced to go in and take my grain.

Dave Senter happened to be staying with us at the time and he was a good friend of mine. He was originally from Texas and had moved to Washington, D.C., to work as a lobbyist for the American Agriculture Movement. I asked if Dave could attend the meeting with me and the bank president said that he would prefer that I come by myself. But I insisted that Dave come along. We set a date and time to meet. The bank president told me that we would meet in a private room at the airport.

Dave and I drove to Memphis and when we got to the airport, we went to the room where we were to hold the meeting. When we walked in, the President of the First Tennessee Bank introduced himself and the other bank officials that were there. The food was great and we were given the "red carpet treatment." They treated us like royalty and just couldn't do enough for us.

After we finished our meal, the president of the bank said, "Mr. Cryts, I think we need to get down to the business at hand. You are costing the First Tennessee Bank a considerable amount of money and causing us some bad publicity. We would like to get this matter resolved and behind us. If you will agree to stop your fight and just back off, The First Tennessee Bank is prepared to make you whole several times over."

He never would mention a dollar figure, but told me several times during the meeting that he was prepared to make me "whole" several times over.

Then, I asked about the other farmers that had grain in the elevator? He said, "The hell with the other farmers. They are not the ones fighting us. Our deal is with you, if you will quit right now, we will make you whole several times over."

I argued, "I've got the largest amount of grain in that elevator and it wouldn't take two or three times what you are offering me to pay off all of them."

Then, he said, "We are not prepared to do that. And we will not do that. We want to make an agreement with you and you only."

I said, "I'm sorry, but I just can't do that. I would not be doing the other farmers right, if I make a deal like this. I just can't do it."

The meeting ended shortly after that. I was amazed that they were willing to pay that much money to me and not the rest of the farmers. We just wanted what was rightfully ours.

They did try to settle with me personally on two separate occasions. I could have agreed to either one of the two deals that I was offered and got out of the middle of the bankruptcy case. In doing so, I would have done very well for my family. But, I just couldn't bring myself to do it. It was not the right thing to do. The other farmers that had grain stored in the elevator were my friends and neighbors, and we were all in this together.

In the mean time, the country had elected Ronald Reagan to be the President of the United States; while Southeast Missouri had elected Bill Emerson as our Representative to the United States Congress. President Regan had run on states rights and wanted to reduce the power of the federal government and give it back to the states. But that didn't help us. The State of Missouri had just fought and lost a real battle for state's rights against a federal judge in Arkansas who claimed jurisdiction over the bankruptcy case involving Missouri farmers.

I really didn't want to go to the elevator and remove the grain for fear of not knowing what would happen. We were so close to getting this problem resolved with the USDA under the Carter Administration that I felt like I had to go back to Washington, D.C., one more time to see if the USDA under a new administration would again consider buying out our loans with the CCC.

I called Representative Bill Emerson's Office and told him that I would like to have a meeting set up with the new people in the U. S. Department of Agriculture. He asked when I wanted the meeting set up and I told him as soon as possible. Representative Emerson told me that he would get it done.

About a week before the date set to remove the grain, I flew to Washington, D.C. When I got there, I expected to meet Representative Emerson, so he could go to the meeting with me. However, he sent one of his aides instead. I had asked Dave Senter to go to the meeting with me, because he was also in the meeting that I had with Congressman Burleson. Dave was a good friend of mine and our AAM lobbyist in Washington, D.C.

Seeley Lodwick and Edward Hughes were the two people that represented the Commodity Credit Corporation in the USDA. When Dave and I walked in, Representative Emerson's aide introduced me to Mr. Lodwick and Mr. Hughes. They said they were somewhat familiar with the problem that we had at the elevator through the news reports. I told them that a similar situation happened to some farmers in Minnesota when their elevators had gone bankrupt. Then, I explained that the Minnesota farmers all had Commodity Credit loans and the Commodity Credit Corporation had bought out their equity in the grain. This had gotten the farmers out of the middle of the bankruptcy case and Commodity Credit took over from there.

They looked at each other and Mr. Hughes said, "We don't have a problem with that. In fact, it sounds like a good idea. We'll get to work on it right away."

I felt like the weight of the world had just been lifted off of my shoulders and that this nightmare was finally almost over.

As Dave and I got up to leave, the door opened. When I saw who walked in, my heart dropped to my stomach. It was Arnold Grundelman, the same legal counsel who had been there under the Carter Administration when I met with Congressman Burleson. I could not believe he was still there.

When he saw me, he started shaking his head, walked over to them, and said, "I know what he wants. It's against legal counsel's advice, and we are not going to do it."

Seeley Lodwick and Edward Hughes looked at each other, and then looked at me. They were surprised and confused. These two men were newly appointed as policy people for the USDA and didn't want to make any mistakes. They told Mr. Grundelman that a precedent had been set in Minnesota when the Commodity Credit bought out the equity of the farmers there to get them out of the middle of the bankruptcy case.

Mr. Grundelman said, "Yes, this has been done before, but we will never do it again."

Since these two guys were new to the USDA, they refused to make a decision that would go against Mr. Grundelman's advice. I was very disappointed when Grundelman refused to let the new administration provide a way out of this mess for us. So, again, with no hope of a resolution, I left Washington, D.C., the next day to go back home.

Trucks begin to arrive at Ramada Inn Headquarters.

Removal of Grain

My family and I went to the Ramada Inn at Sikeston where we set up headquarters to begin making plans to remove the grain. When we got there, we were overwhelmed with the number of phone calls that we were getting. People from all over the country were calling to let us know they were coming to help us remove our grain. Some of them were actually driving their grain trucks here to help haul the grain out of the elevator. Someone in Nebraska sent us an article that read,

"A group of farmers were seen leaving Lincoln, Nebraska, this morning headed to Southeast Missouri to help Puxico Farmer Wayne Cryts remove his grain from the elevator. They left with an American Flag in one hand and a scoop shovel in the other."

As people started arriving in Sikeston, they would come to our headquarters to find out what they could do to help. As I was talking to them, I was surprised to find out that they were not there just to support me personally, but to help fight an unjust law. They could not believe that a judge could order someone's private property to be sold to help pay another person's debt.

By this time, I was beginning to feel like the dog that caught the moving car—this situation was getting bigger than I ever imagined it would. It was so overwhelming that I began to wonder how we were going to handle it all. There was an estimated three to four thousand people from thirty-five states that had come to be a part of "B-Day" or "Bean Day" as some people were calling it.

On Friday before "Bean Day," my dad and I went to the Risco State bank to visit with Van Gibbs, who was the bank president, and told him that we were going to the ASCS office to pay off the CCC loan on the grain. Van told us to go ahead and write the check, and the bank would honor it. We could fill out the paperwork later.

Then, we went to the ASCS office to pay off the loan, but Larry Blunt, the local ASCS director, told us that he could not accept a check for the loan. He did not say why he would not accept a check, so we left and went back to the motel. We decided that we would just pay them with cash later.

Wayne addresses supporters at Rally.

Wayne meets with Law Enforcement officials to outline plans to remove the grain.

After we removed our grain from the Ristine Elevator, we planned to take the grain to the MFA Elevator in Bernie and sell it. Then, we would have enough cash to pay the CCC loan.

The next day, I decided that the first thing I needed to do was to set up a meeting with the Missouri State Highway Patrol. I called the Highway Patrol Headquarters in Sikeston Saturday afternoon. I told them who I was and asked to speak to the officer-in-charge. I was connected to Lt. Joe Faber and he asked how he could help me? I told him that I would like to meet with him.

He said, "Wayne, I am so glad you called. When and where would you like to meet? We need to talk!"

I asked Lt. Faber if we could meet Sunday afternoon, the next day, at four o'clock in his office. He said that would be fine. He would be there waiting for me.

I also told him, "I'm having a rally this evening and planned to tell those attending the rally about our meeting with you tomorrow. I will ask for a spokesman from each state to meet with me after the rally. I would like to have them meet with you as well, if you think it would be all right."

He said, "That would be great."

I also invited the Missouri Highway Patrol, the FBI, and the federal marshals to attend the rally that evening as well, because I wanted everybody to understand what was going to happen when we removed our grain on Monday. And I wanted everybody to know that if anyone got out of line, started a ruckus with law enforcement officers or anybody else, that he or she would not be considered part of my group.

After the rally, I informed the people that law enforcement officers could arrest them and do whatever they want to do with them, if there was any violence. Again, I emphasized this point several times. I did not want any guns or weapons of any kind brought to the elevator. I asked everyone to keep themselves under control and if need be, keep the person beside them under control. I thanked them for the help, support, and cooperation. Then, I told them that I wanted everyone to divide into groups by the state that they came from and pick a representative that would meet with me after the rally. At that meeting, I explained to them that I had set up a meeting the next day at 4:00 p.m. with the Missouri State Troopers at Highway Patrol Headquarters, because I wanted everybody to know exactly what was going on and what was said.

After the rally, the highway patrol officers and federal marshals asked me if I was serious about what I had just said? I told them that I was very serious, but I did not want them to go out of their way to arrest someone either. I reassured them that I did not want any violence and if anybody starts any kind of trouble that threatens the safety of this process, that they can arrest him, take him to jail, and he was on his own.

The next day at four o'clock, we went down to troop headquarters to meet with the state troopers. When we walked in, I was met by Major Clarence E. Fisher who was from the Missouri Highway Patrol Headquarters in Jefferson City and Captain Richard D. Radford who was the Commander of Troop E Headquarters in Poplar Bluff.

Captain Radford said, "Mr. Cryts, we are concerned about safety on the highway. And, I want you to know up front that we have Howard Safir, Assistant Director of Operations with the U.S. Marshals Service in Washington, D.C., and Deputy U.S. Marshal Larry Strahorn with the U.S. Marshals Office in St. Louis, and several FBI agents sitting in this meeting. Is that all right with you?"

I said, "Yes sir, I'm glad to have them here."

Captain Radford asked, "Wayne, what are your plans for Monday morning?"

I told him that I planned to go to the elevator Monday morning at ten o'clock and start loading grain. Then, I saw a blackboard located in front of the room, so I asked if I could use it. The Captain said that would be fine, so I began by drawing the layout of the area where the elevator was located. Then, I drew the highway that we would be on as we drove to the elevator. I told them, "Once we get to the elevator, we will turn into the entrance by the scale and wait until 10:00 a.m. before we enter the property. Our grain trucks will be loaded with farmers who would be there to assist us. After the meeting is over with today, we are going to have approximately ten trucks coming down to hotel headquarters. The rest of the trucks are going to go on down to the elevator and park along this gravel road beside the elevator, so we won't have so much congestion on the highway in the morning. We plan to have around 80 trucks there, ready to load the grain. Some of the trucks will have license plates on them from other states."

Then, I explained, "There are five storage bins that have a concrete foundation with an arched roof made of tin. We will gain access to the grain by loosening the tin over the storage bins. Then, we will remove approximately 33,000 bushels of soybeans that are stored in bins 1, 4, and 5. We will have trucks waiting outside to be loaded with the equipment that I will bring in myself. The trucks will be weighed empty as they enter the facility and again when they are loaded. When we have removed our grain from the storage bins, we will replace the tin on the roof and clean up the facility."

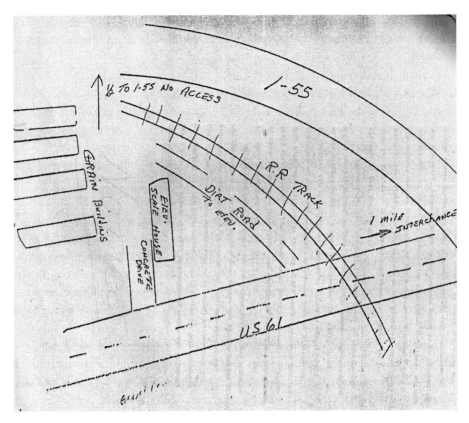

FBI replicated Wayne's chalkboard diagram of plans to enter the Ristine Elevator.

I also made it clear to everyone in the meeting that I would not tolerate any violence during this whole operation. I told them that I had made it clear to all of the people there supporting me that they are to obey any reasonable request for public safety. In addition, I informed them that the actions taking place the next day was not an official function of the American Agriculture Movement although many who do support that movement would be there supporting me. Then, I told them that anyone outside of the Ristine Elevator area that got involved in any improper actions would not be considered part of my group and I would expect the Missouri Highway Patrol to handle him in their normal procedures.

Next, I introduced Dave Senter and Marvin Meeks to them and informed them that theses two men have an 8:00 a.m. meeting in Washington, D.C., the next day with the Secretary of Agriculture. I said, "These two guys would be leaving tonight for one last chance to try to work out and agreement with the government. If they can get an acceptable agreement at any point during the day, they will call me and I will stop the removal of grain until we find out if it is acceptable or not."

Captain Radford told me that I could have Dave or Marvin call the Troop E satellite station in Sikeston, if they could reach an agreement for us to consider. Then, the state troopers would radio the message over to their people at the elevator who would get the message to us so we could stop what we were doing to consider the agreement.

I concluded by saying, "If I am served court papers from federal officials, I will accept them and proceed to remove my grain. If I am arrested, I will go to jail peacefully."

Alvin Jenkins, from Campo Colorado, stood up and said, "Even if Wayne Cryts is arrested, I am going to get some beans out of that elevator for my friend. If they hit me on the head, I will not fight back. If they arrest me, I will go to jail."

Many other farmers vowed that if the law enforcement officials tried to arrest just a few farmers to set an example, they should plan on finding enough jail space to hold all of them.

Captain Radford said, "We have been getting messages from law enforcement officers from different states reporting that people from all over the country are headed this way. We are expecting several thousand people to be at the elevator and many of them were already starting to arrive in Sikeston."

I told the Captain, "I think most of the people who are going to be here will arrive this weekend."

He asked, "Who are all these people?"

"I don't know their names, but they are coming to support me when I remove my private property from the elevator."

Captain Radford said, "Wayne, what are we going to do if there are so many people here that we can't accommodate them? Can we set up a road block and let all the grain trucks through and then start turning everyone else back?"

I said, "Captain Radford, the problem that we are going to have is this: if there is a farmer or someone else that has driven here from Nebraska, Wyoming, Minnesota, or some other state who is here to support me and he is met by a road block, he may think that something went wrong and may just try to bust through the road block."

He said, "What do you suggest that we do?"

I said, "Well, I don't want anybody to get hurt. So, I'll put one of my AAM friends with you at the road block, and if it is a sightseer or someone that has no business coming down here, then you can turn them back. But, if it is a farmer, you let them on through. Even if they have to park somewhere and walk, let them through."

Captain Radford agreed to this. I felt like this agreement would cut down congestion and keep traffic flowing. Captain Radford reported that they had twenty-five cars ready to respond if needed.

On Monday morning, just as we were getting ready to leave hotel headquarters, the telephone rang and one of my friends answered the phone. It was a lawyer that had been following the story and asked to speak to Wayne Cryts. The farmer that answered the phone told him that I was getting ready to leave. I never found out who the lawyer was, but he told the farmer that he specialized in constitution law and he had called to give Wayne some advice. He told that farmer to get a pen and something to write on. So, the farmer picked up a pen and a hotel napkin and wrote down what the lawyer said.

Then, the lawyer said, "Be sure to tell Wayne that if they read a court order to him this morning that he should read this back to them."

Supporters await Wayne Cryts convoy to arrive at the elevator.

The farmer stuck the napkin in his pocket and hurried out to find me. My family and I were just getting in the truck to leave when that farmer came running out the door hollering, "Wayne, Wayne, Wayne! A constitution lawyer just called and told me to write this down and give it to you."

He took the hotel napkin out of his pocket and handed it to me. I took the napkin and read it out loud, so Sandy and the kids could hear it. It said, "Your court order was written under equity law. I am a sovereign individual and a citizen of the State of Missouri operating under common law, therefore your court order has no weight of law nor does it have jurisdiction over me." Then, I stuck it in my pocket and didn't think anything else about it.

A line of federal marshals awaits Cryts Convoy.

I looked around to see if all the drivers were ready to go. We had decided to leave a little earlier than we had previously planned, because it was sprinkling rain and so foggy that I could hardly see ten feet in front of me. I leaned over, kissed Sandy, and told her and the kids that I loved them very much.

I started the truck and we led our convoy down the road to the highway toward the Ristine Elevator. When we were about three miles away from the elevator, we saw a state trooper's car sitting in every driveway and side road along the way. When I turned off the highway onto the road that went to the Ristine Elevator, I anticipated that everybody would be there waiting outside the elevator for us to arrive. Then, I would enter the James Brothers' property and the people that were there to support me would come in behind me. But, when I pulled in on the driveway, there were a lot of the farmers already scattered throughout the elevator property and that kind of worried me. However, Sandy was relieved to see that they had not put a chain across the entrance, so we did not have to force our way in to the property.

As I drove toward the elevator, I saw a line of federal marshal's blocking the entrance. So, I stopped the convoy of trucks, opened the door, and stepped out on the running board to see who was behind them. I could see that the FBI had lined up behind the federal marshals and that there were some deputy sheriffs mixed in with them.

I looked at my watch and it was 9:35 a.m. We got there a little early, because we did not want to be rushed due to the rain and fog. We had twenty-five minutes to sit there and wait. I did not want to enter the property before 10:00 a.m. since that was the time that I had set in my press conference. I began to think about what could happen if anything went wrong. I knew they could consider the truck a deadly weapon when we started driving toward them, and we could be injured or killed.

Then, while I waited, I began thinking about my childhood and growing up on the family farm. It had a major impact on who I was and what I was doing, causing me to be at this turning point in my life.

I was born on August 25th 1946, in Dexter, Missouri. My dad's name is William H. Cryts, Sr. and my mother's name is Geneva Etoil Cryts. I have a brother that is three years older than me, and his name is William Earl Cryts. We called him "Bill." Later on, we had a younger sister whose name is LeAnn. My Grandpa and Grandma Cryts lived across the woods from us. They had been farming all their lives too. We had a path between our house and theirs and we would go visit them most every day. Our family was very close and when anyone needed help, someone was there ready to assist us.

In 1952, my dad bought two hundred acres of wooded land in New Madrid for twenty dollars an acre from George Bader. The contract stated that Dad had to clear and put in production at least forty acres of land per year for five years or all the land would revert back to George. So, we began clearing the land to prepare it for farming. I was six years old at the time. New Madrid was an hour's drive from our home just outside of Dexter. So, we lived in an old tar shack with no running water or electricity during the week, while we cleared the land. The mosquitoes were so bad at night that my brother and I always had a hard time going to sleep. So, my dad would put my brother and me on the back of the log truck and drive us up and down the road to keep the mosquitoes off of us until we went to sleep.

My dad dozed down the trees and pushed them into rows. Then, we cut blocks out of the trees and put them aside to be hauled to town. My brother and I picked up the tree branches and roots that the dozer missed and threw them on the piles. Then, I would carry a can of diesel fuel around, dump fuel on the piles, and burn them. Another one of my jobs was to pick up the chunks that were left in the field and put them in a pile to be burned. Chunks are pieces of wood and debris on the field that had to be picked up before crops could be planted.

On Saturdays, we would haul a load of blocks to IXL in Dexter. Lavern Keithley owned IXL. I think he admired my dad for being such an honest hardworking man. The following Monday morning, we would go by on our way to the farm in New Madrid and pick up a check from Mr. Keithley for the blocks. I remember hearing my dad tell us that it seemed like the check was a little too much. Mr. Keithley knew that the money we got from selling the blocks was all we had to live and farm on from week to week. We had to use the money that we received from selling the crops to pay on our loan each year to Mr. Bader.

One summer, the flood came so late that it ruined our crops and my dad could not make the third payment to Mr. Bader. Herlis Cox had a small business in Dexter and my dad was telling him about it. So, Herlis asked dad how much he needed to make his payment and dad told him. Herlis went to the back of the store and came back with the money. They just shook hands for the loan and that was all that was necessary. The next fall, my dad paid him back in full.

At the end of the five years, my dad went to see George to make the final payment for the two hundred acres of land. I remember hearing George tell my dad that he would never have sold him the land if he had thought he could have cleared the land and put it into production. He said, "You are a hard workingman with a good family, Mr. Cryts."

I always had chores to do as I was growing up, even when I was real little. We didn't have running water in the house, but we had a water faucet outside and I was supposed to keep the water bucket full at all times. We also had twelve milk cows that had to be milked by hand every day, morning and night. Back then, when a little kid first started learning to milk, he was given a small lard can to milk in to. So, I got my little can and took off to the barn with my dad and grandpa. My goal was to be able to fill up my little can before they could fill up their big buckets, so they would know that I was grown up and needed a big bucket just like them. While my grandpa was taking the buckets up to the house to separate the milk from the cream, I would slip up behind him and pour my milk into his bucket. That way, I could tell grandma that I worked hard too and she wouldn't know that I only had my little can half full. I wanted her to be proud of me for working hard like my dad and grandpa.

We also raised a lot of cotton and at harvest time, the adults had a long pick sack that they picked cotton in. The little kids took a small tow sack with a piece of cloth attached to it to put around our neck. Then, we would work as hard as we could to fill up that little tow sack. My goal was to try to get enough cotton in the tow sack to convince them that I needed a big pick sack like they had. I always worked hard to show my dad and my grandpa that I was grown up.

I remember watching the Rural Electric Association wire our house for electricity. We were only allowed one light bulb in a room and one plug in. They did not have the capacity to put more outlets in the house at that time. But, we really didn't need any more than that because we did not have televisions, refrigerators, or other household appliances. A radio was the only thing that we used the outlet for in the living room.

I can remember the first television that came into our area. We had neighbors down the road by the name of Fleeman. They got the first television and every Saturday night Mom would fix us our special meal of hamburgers and French fries with a Pepsi to drink. Then, we would go down to the Fleemans and watch television.

We had a lot of kids in the neighborhood and when we were not working, we would go down to the creek to swim. We also had corncob fights in the barn, played "kick the can" and "hide and go seek." The neighbors visited with each other a lot back then.

We went to church every Sunday. Sometimes kids would start cutting up. If their parents didn't get on to them right away, the other people that went to church would correct the child. We were taught to respect our elders and behave when we were in public.

One day, Grandpa, Dad, and I were going to the country store. I was so eager to get in there, because Grandpa had given me a nickel to buy a soda. I was in such a hurry to get in there that I ran in front of an elderly man as he was getting ready to go through the door. My dad came in, grabbed me by the hair of the head, and dragged me back out the door.

He said, "Son, you never run in front of an older person. That is very disrespectful."

I never forgot that and I certainly didn't feel abused. I never ran in front of another person again and I've always respected other people.

Back then, we knew if we did something wrong, we were going to get our tail busted over it. We didn't get mad at our parents about it; we just knew it was going to happen. My grandparents also had a lot of influence on my life back then and I certainly didn't want to disappoint them either. I had a tremendous amount of respect for both my parents and my grandparents.

I went to school in a one-room schoolhouse until I was in the seventh grade. Then, I went to school in Dexter, Missouri. Leroy Stafford was my best friend growing up. We were classmates and he also worked on the farm each summer with me for my dad. Leroy would miss a month or two of school each year, because his family would go to Florida at harvest time to pick fruit and vegetables.

I went with my friends to the roller rink every chance I got and considered myself a good skater. We would put chairs out in the floor and jump them. I could also skate backward and do figure 8's along with other maneuvers. One Saturday evening when I was at the roller rink putting my skates on, I saw this girl skating around out there. I was fourteen years old at the time and this was the first time that I had seen her. I don't know what it was, but there was just something about her that really intrigued me. I wanted to impress her, so I would go around skating backward, doing crazy eights, and anything else I thought she might like. Finally, I went up and asked her if she would skate with me. She said, "No, I'm not about to skate with you!" Later on, she told me that I was the biggest showoff she had ever seen.

Even though she had turned me down, I was determined to get to know her. So, I came up behind her, put the toe of my skate out, caught the back wheel of her skate, and tripped her without her knowing it. She fell down and I very gallantly stopped and offered to pick her up. I took her by the hands. She kind of tugged, trying to get away from me, but I helped her up anyway. I started skating around with her and she allowed me to do so for a while. Then, I asked her what her name was and where she was from. She told me her name was Sandy and that she was from Puxico, and then she went home.

The next day, I asked my friend, Terry Fletcher, if he would take me to Puxico to see if we could find Sandy. As we were coming into town, we saw that they were having a rodeo there. We decided to stop and watch it for a while. And by chance or fate, as I would like to think, I spotted Sandy and we talked for quite a while. I also find out that another friend of mine, Wayne Moore, was going out with her sister, Bonnie. So, I asked Sandy if she would go out with me. She said, "No, my dad won't let me go out."

Later, I found out that the next weekend my friend Wayne was going up to see Bonnie. So, I decided to tag along with him. Wayne was going to take Bonnie to Jones's where teenagers went to hang out. When we got to their house, Mr. Hyten, Bonnie and Sandy's dad, was standing in the doorway.

I went up to him and said, "Mr. Hyten, I would like to take your daughter up to Jones's with Bonnie and Wayne."

He looked at me real stern and said, "Hell boy, you ain't taking my daughter nowhere."

So, I just went over and set down on the couch. I couldn't go any where else since I was with Wayne. We were all just sitting there and it was pretty quiet. Finally, her dad decided that we could go to Jones's with Wayne and Bonnie, but we could only stay thirty or forty minutes.

When I got my driver's license, I asked my dad if I could borrow the pickup truck to go out with Sandy. My dad only had a pickup and a log truck and he had to have the pickup that day. So, I had to drive the old log truck. We went to a drive-in theater on our first real date.

I took this old log truck on several of our dates. It had been turned over once and damaged. All the glass was broke out of it, the door wouldn't close, and it had a log chain wrapped around the back of the cab to hold the doors closed. The gas tank had rusted out, so we had two five-gallon cans that we just set in the floorboard of the truck and ran a hose to the fuel pump. When the truck was about ready to run out of gas in one can, I would tell Sandy to switch cans. She was so quick at it that the old truck never missed a stroke. I actually admired her for that.

The brakes didn't work either. One afternoon I decided that I wanted to go see Sandy, so I drove the old log truck up to her house. When I was pulling up in the yard, I saw her dad standing on the porch. I couldn't get the truck stopped and ran into one of his shade trees. He just looked at me and shook his head. I don't think Sandy married me for my truck!

Sandy was a year older than me and when she graduated, she went to work at a factory in Bloomfield, Missouri. I graduated in May of the following year at age seventeen. Sandy and I got married in July. I tell everybody, we got married, left on our honeymoon, and we never got back. It's been an unbelievable marriage and an unbelievable partnership.

My best friend, Leroy Stafford, was working on the farm with me one summer and he carved a heart in a cottonwood tree with Sandy and my name in it. Shortly after that, he was drafted into the Army. When he finished basic training, he was given orders to go to Vietnam. Leroy told Sandy and me that he would not be coming back home. We told him not to think that way and he said, "No Wayne, I won't be back." Two weeks after he got to Vietnam, Leroy was shot in the stomach and passed away. The old cottonwood tree on our family farm that he carved our names in meant the world to me, because he was like a brother to me.

I never had any intention of doing anything but farming. College didn't interest me whatsoever. I always knew that I was going to be a farmer. I had served as an apprentice with my dad and grandpa ever since I was old enough to walk. Sandy and I bought a farm in Puxico and went into farming with my dad and brother. We had a three family farm operation and partnership. We had land at New Madrid and rented an 800 acre farm in Kewanee. We kept expanding our farming operation until we were farming about 2,300 acres.

My dad had a caterpillar dozer that he used to clear the land. He also had ulcers that bothered him a lot due to worrying about whether or not we would have a good harvest. I remember his ulcers would hurt him so bad that at times he would have to shut the dozer off and roll on the ground until it would ease up. We worked hard for everything we had.

When my son Terry was born, he had the same desire that I had with my dad and grandpa. He wanted to work side by side with us from the time he was old enough to walk. He was always involved in the farming operation. And when I think back to where my strong work ethic came from, it was working with my dad and grandpa and wanting to make them proud of me.

I was in the front of the house working on our 4020 John Deere tractor one day and heard some pecking on the other side. I walked around the tractor to see what it was. I saw Terry, just a little ol' thing, there with a hammer pecking on the tractor too. He wanted to be just like me. I was as proud as any dad could be of his son.

Later that day, we went into a little country store to pick up a few things and I had some grease and dirt on me. Someone said, "Wayne, it looks like you have really been working hard." I noticed that every time after that day, when we were out working and needed to go to the country store, Terry would get some grease or dirt and rub it on him. He wanted everybody to know, just like I did back when I milked cows and picked cotton as a boy, that he was working hard too.

When our daughter, Paula, was old enough to work, she started driving a tractor and working on the farm too. We had a real family farm operation. We usually started harvesting the grain at New Madrid in late October. My wife, Sandy, was one of our main truck drivers. She can tell you many stories of her experiences driving the "old blue goose." It was very hard to drive. It didn't have power steering or power brakes. In fact, it had vacuum assist brakes that would only work when the engine was running. Having an old truck seems to run in the family.

I'll never forget one of our nieces riding with Sandy to deposit a load of grain at the Ristine Elevator. The floor was rusted out on the passenger side and my niece, Angel Moore, could see the wheel spinning as they went down the road and that really fascinated her. From that day on, she always wanted to ride with Sandy in the "old blue goose," so she could watch the wheels turning.

The Confrontation

I kept looking at my watch. It just kept ticking down slowly, one minute at a time. At ten o'clock, Sandy reached over, took my hand, and said, "Are you ready?"

I said, "Yes, I'm ready."

Paula was sitting next to Sandy, and, by this time, Terry was in the back of the truck with the other farmers. Herman Linville was standing on the running board hanging on the side of the truck. The trucks that were behind us were loaded with farmers and ready to proceed.

It was time for us to get this operation under way. I got out of the truck and walked up to the eight federal marshals that were lined up in front of me. Then, Howard Safir from the U.S. Marshals Office in Washington, D.C., pulled out a court order and read it to me. The court order forbade me from coming in and removing the grain. When he was done reading it, he told me that any attempt by those involved to take the grain or to impede or obstruct the U.S. Marshals in the performance of their duties to protect the facilities and the property therein was a felony and we would be prosecuted under the criminal laws of the United States.

At that moment, I remembered the napkin that the farmer had given me that morning. So, I reached in my pocket and pulled out the napkin. I had no idea if it meant anything or not, but I didn't think it could hurt either. I stated my name and said, "Your court order was written under equity law. I am a sovereign individual and a citizen of the State of Missouri operating under common law; therefore, your court order has no weight of law against me nor does it have jurisdiction over me."

They just looked at me like, O.K. Then, they handed me the court order and I handed them my napkin. I went down the row, shook hands with everybody, and walked back to my truck. The marshals talked to each other a few minutes while I walked back to my truck.

I got in, started it up, put it in granny low, let out on the clutch, and started driving toward them. Terry was still in back of the truck with the other farmers.

Sandy and Paula closed their eyes and put their heads down. They were so scared that they could not look.

Federal marshal reads court order to Cryts.

I kept moving toward the marshals very slowly and just as I got to them, U.S. Deputy Marshal Larry Strahorn said, "Boys, we better get our butts out of the way," and they parted like the Red Sea. Then, I pulled in on the scales.

A little over a year after this event, I read an article in the Wall Street Journal dated May 12, 1982, written by Lynda Schuster where she quoted U.S. Federal Marshal Howard Safir as saying, "Based on intelligence, we believed the farmers were willing and able to fight. My concern was some folks would be killed, primarily some farmers. It didn't warrant killing people over basically a civil dispute." Marshal Safir also stated that he was told to use his own judgment to assess the situation and to make sure no one got hurt.

You cannot imagine the tension that everyone was feeling. Alvin Jenkins, who was on the front fender, stood up and said, "Let's go get them beans."

Everybody there began to shout and cheer. There was an estimated three to four thousand people there to support my right to remove my private property that I had title to, and the volume of noise was getting louder and louder.

Marshal Strahorn said, "Boys, we better get our butts out of the way."

When I got out of the truck, I could see that the federal marshals and FBI Agents were getting worried about what was going to happen next. So, I stood up on the running board and hollered, "Everybody just quiet down for a minute! Let's take a fifteen minute break. Everybody just calm down and we will get ready to go to the next step, but let's just everybody settle down."

Everybody just started talking to each other. That was the first time I met Glen Young. He walked up to me and said, "Mr. Cryts, I'm Glen Young. I'm head of the FBI in the State of Missouri. Would you meet with us in the back office? We would like to talk to you." I agreed.

When I went in the office, the first thing Mr. Young said was, "Mr. Cryts, you have taken possession of this facility. We would like your permission to remain on the site."

I was shocked when he asked me that, because I thought he was going to arrest me or something. I replied, "Sure, that's fine with me."

Trying to gather further information on the situation, Mr. Young then asked, "How many farmers were going to remove their grain?"

"I am the only one. The others have backed out."

Then, he asked, "What are you going to do next?"

"I plan to bring in my weight and measure crew that are considered experts. One man is Homer Evens from Ulysses, Kansas, who has been managing a Bunge elevator for more than twenty years. The other man is Corky Jones who owns his own elevator in Brownville, Nebraska."

I brought both of these men in and introduced them as my weigh-in crew. In order to make sure that we do everything right as we remove my grain, these men have to weigh, probe, and figure foreign material. When I had brought my grain in for storage, it also had foreign material in it. So, I wanted to make sure that I took out exactly what I brought in.

My grain was stored in three different Quonset Huts and I planned to remove approximately one third of my grain from each one. By doing this, I would be removing approximately the same quality of grain as I brought in. I also planned to leave one hundred bushels of my grain in each of those bins just in case the scale was off. I did not want to take a chance of removing a bushel more than I actually owned, because all I had wanted since the beginning was to get my private property back, so I could sell the grain and pay my bills. I would rather leave one hundred bushels in each bin than take more than what was mine.

Grain stored in Quonset huts.

I told Glen that we had brought elevators, vacuators, and everything that we needed to load the grain in my trucks. When the trucks were loaded, I planned to line the trucks up so we could all leave together.

He said, "Mr. Cryts, I want you to understand that we are going to be gathering evidence during this whole process. And, if we think we have enough evidence for an arrest, you and others may be arrested today. We will also follow the trucks when you leave here today and if we are ordered to seize the grain, the trucks will be seized as well."

Farmers open grain bin.

I told him that I understood what he was telling me. He said, "All right."

Then, he told me that Special Agent Marshall Gorham would be stationed at the scales observing and making record of the weight of the trucks. I told him that would be fine with me.

When we went back outside, I announced to everyone what Glen had told me. I informed those that were there to support me that the FBI would be taking pictures, gathering evidence, and possible charges might be filed against us. And if they were told to seize the grain, the trucks would be seized as well. After that was finished, we were ready to get set up to remove the beans.

Wayne ecstatic about regaining possession of his private property while holding the Nebraska scoop shovel.

It was still raining as we unloaded the equipment out of the trucks and set it in place. Next, we removed some sheets of tin on the storage facility and set up our elevators. Then, we attached a vacuator, which is a huge vacuum cleaner with a suction pipe that sucks the beans out of the bin and dumps it over in the truck. By the time we got the tin removed and all the equipment set in place to begin removing the grain, it was almost eleven o'clock. We moved my truck into place and began loading it. By the time we had finished loading the first truck, the rain had stopped. Then, we drove the truck up on the scales to weigh it. Clarence Parks, an employee at the Ristine Elevator, began adjusting the scales. From that time on, I spent just about all my time that day in the office with the federal authorities. The FBI agents were wearing plain clothes trying to blend in and look like the rest of us. My son, Terry, was helping in the grain bins, while Sandy and Paula helped with the food.

The federal agents put a tremendous amount of pressure on me, trying to get me to stop what we were doing and drive away. They had two chairs set up along one side of the office. I sat in one chair and Glen usually set in the other. There were other FBI Agents there that day. Some of their names were Special Agents Norman Christensen, Homer Hoffman, James Lummus, Marshall Gorham, Ronald Parker, Richard Kneibert, Frank Pasieka, Herman Nichols, Marvin Pennington, and Richard Herman. While I was in the office with Special Agent Glen Young, some of these guys were walking around, starring at me, and trying to intimidate me. They would play good cop/bad cop like you see on television.

Glen was the good cop, and he would put his arm around me and tell me that he understood what I was going through. He would say, "Wayne, you have got to understand what you are doing and the consequences of your actions."

Then, there would be another agent playing the bad guy and he would say, "Wayne, you are going to get people killed. They are your friends and supporters, and we know that you don't want to get any of them harmed. That would be on your conscience for the rest of your life. You are going to prison for this. You know that, don't you?"

One would bring me up and the other would crash me. It went back and forth like that the whole day. There were times when I got so emotional that I wanted to stop, but I would remember that this was a family decision and we had decided to follow it through to the end.

Occasionally, there would be a problem out there and a farmer would open the door, come in, and say, "Wayne, we have a problem." I would go look at it, make the best decision that I could, and go back in the office. Then, the federal authorities would start back in on me again.

At about five or five thirty that evening, it was getting dark and I was exhausted. By that time, fifty trucks had been loaded. I said, "Glen, I tell you what I would like to do. If you give me your word that we won't have to fight to get back in here in the morning, I would like to shut the operation down. I'll tell everybody to go back up to the motel, clean up, get something to eat, and get a good night's rest. Because the darker it gets, the more tired everybody will get, and the more chances we will have of problems developing. Besides, I don't know all the people that are here."

He said, "Wayne, let me do some calling."

He went out to the front office to make some phone calls. Then, he came back in and said, "Wayne, you have our word. You can shut the operation down and start back in the morning right where you are now."

I went outside and told everyone what we were going to do. Then, we shut the operation down and went back to the motel in Sikeston.

Later that evening at the motel, some of the federal officers came in to our room to talk to us. They set down and we began to talk about things that happened that day. One of them said, "Wayne, we can see what your biggest problem is, Judge Baker is a prick. We just finished talking to him on the phone and he has threatened to arrest us for 'contempt of court' for not upholding his court order."

I told them about the time that I had requested to speak to him at one of the court hearings. He sent a message back informing me that he didn't want to speak to Wayne Cryts or any of those damn farmers.

I think they began to understand what we were going through with the judge. After a couple of hours of talking about other problems we had with Judge Baker, we decided that we had better go to bed and try to get some sleep. However, I didn't sleep a wink that night.

We went back to the elevator the next the morning at daylight. We got everyone in place and started loading the trucks again. Somewhere around 1:30 or 2:00 that afternoon, Glen Young and several other federal officers came in the office, lined up around the wall, and looked down at me. I was sitting in a chair talking to one of the FBI agents.

Glen said, "Wayne, you have gone as far as you are going to go. Orders have come down for us to stop you. We do not have a choice. You have got to understand that you are responsible if anyone gets hurt or killed. You will suffer the penalty for that. What are you going to do? We need your answer now."

You can't imagine what that did to me, because I knew they were serious. For the first time, since we started removing the grain, I didn't know what to do. I could feel myself getting ready to collapse. I was mentally and physically exhausted. Finally, I said, "Glen, would you do me a favor?"

"What is it, Wayne?"

"Glen, would you clear the room and leave me alone for a few minutes, so I can collect my thoughts?"

"Yes, Wayne, I will do that for you."

He told everyone to leave the room. When they closed that door, I fell to pieces. I literally broke down and cried for a solid thirty minutes. I had not slept in three days and was running on fumes. The FBI agents had been continually increasing the pressure on me throughout these two days. One cannot imagine the emotional strain that I had been under. When I finally stopped crying, I felt somewhat refreshed. It helped relieve much of the stress and hopelessness that I had been feeling at the time.

Finally, I made up my mind about what I was going to do and ran it through my mind a few times. I decided to tell Glen that I am going to go outside and thank everyone for being there to help me and providing their support. I will tell them they went far beyond the call of duty. We came here to get my grain and we proved that we could do that. But, the FBI and federal marshals told me that they have been given orders to stop me and we need to realize that they can stop us anytime they want to. Everyone knows that I do not nor did not want anybody hurt, killed, or involved in violence of any kind and that I want them to do what I ask them to do. I will tell the farmers that I plan to take one load of my grain out of this elevator. I am going to get in my truck, put it in low gear, and start for that highway. I don't care what they put in front of me, but I am going to go as far as I can go. When I get to a point that I can't go any further and I have done all I can do, then there will be no feelings of failure. I will know in my heart that I have done everything that I can possibly do to try to save my family farm.

After I composed myself, I knocked on the door and Glen opened it. I was surprised at the look on the agents' faces. They came back in and Glen gave me the biggest hug and patted me on the back. I assume that they must have heard me crying, because they seemed to be very sympathetic to me at this point. There were other federal marshals and FBI agents in the room at that time as well. It was a very emotional time for us. Glen continued to hug me and I could tell that they were caught up in this thing too. Finally, we both took a deep breath. Then, I sat down in my chair and Glen sat on the edge of the desk.

He just sat there looking at me for a while. Finally, he said, "Wayne, I still need your answer. What are you going to do?"

Suddenly, an idea came to me. I looked up at Glen and said without cracking a smile, "Have you ever watched the television show, *The Dukes of Hazzard?*"

He sat there for a few minutes and I think he began to visualize what would happen if everybody jumped in those trucks, pickups, and cars and started tearing out of there. He took his fist, hit that desk, and said, "I have to call D.C. again."

They went back to the outer office again for about fifteen minutes or so to make another phone call. I just sat there waiting for him. Finally, they all came back in, no one sat down, and they lined up along the wall.

Glen walked over to me and said, "Wayne, is that your final decision?"

I came so close to just giving up and calling it quits. But, I looked Glen straight in the eyes and said, "Yes Glen, that's my final decision."

He just stood there looking at me, and then he grinned, shrugged his shoulders, and said, "You are free to go. There will be no arrests made today."

I could not believe he said that, because I was so close to giving up. When Glen told me that there would be no arrests made, I was so overwhelmed with excitement that I could have kissed his feet right there. I went bouncing outside to the scale to tell everyone that we were getting ready to leave.

I was surprised to see my Sunday school teacher, Jessie Deardorff's truck, setting on the scale getting weighed. At that moment I thought to myself, "Most of these people have no idea how close we all were to getting arrested." So, I turned around and walked back in the office. Glen was still in there talking with the other federal officers.

As I walked up to him, I could hear the agents making preparations to follow the trucks. I said, "Glen, I need an agreement with you and I want it in writing."

He said, "What do you need now, Wayne?"

I said, "When this convoy of trucks is ready to leave here today, you draw a line across the road. Everyone that drives a truck out of here across that line will agree to give you his name as he leaves. For those that do not cross the line, then you will forget that they have ever been here. In addition, if there is a farmer that has a truckload of grain and he decides not to drive his truck out of here, then you won't hold him responsible if someone else drives his truck out of here. Only the driver of the truck will be responsible for driving across that line. Finally, if there are not enough drivers willing to drive all these trucks out of here, then that grain will be weighed and put back in the elevator. The only exception that I ask is for the juveniles. My kids came here with me and they will be going out with me. I don't want them to be charged with anything. We will make all the repairs to the storage bins and clean everything up after the trucks have left."

Glen said, "Wayne, I'm not sure that I can do that. Let me get on the phone and see what I can do."

He called someone in D.C. and talked for quite some time before he was able to get it approved. Then, he wrote out the agreement and we signed it. Howard Safir from the U.S. Marshals Office also signed it, and I had a notary public come in, witness it, and put the official seal on it.

When we finished, Glen walked outside, got his car, brought it to the front of the elevator, and parked it. He told me that his car would be considered the magic line. There was a loud speaker on the car and he handed me the microphone. I asked all the farmers to gather around me so I could read them the agreement. I read it to them word for word, as it had been written out and agreed to.

Then, I explained it to them, because I wanted everyone to understand what would happen to anyone who crossed the line and drove a truck full of grain out of here. I told them that each driver will be required to stop, get out of the truck, give his name to an FBI Agent, and get his picture taken. And that anyone who had been here, but decided not to drive their truck out of here would be forgotten. It would be as though he had never been here and would not be charged with anything. I also explained to them that if they had a truck here that was loaded with grain and didn't want to cross the line, the owner of the truck would not be responsible if someone else drove his truck out of here. I made absolutely sure that everyone understood the agreement.

After we got this process over and everybody understood it, we gave each truck owner some time to think about the agreement before we pulled out. I had one of my friends count the number of trucks that were ready to leave and he told me we had 78 trucks in line, but one was not needed. So, we had 77 trucks full of grain and ready to go.

The person responsible for getting most of the grain trucks that we used at the elevator was Quincy Murphy. I thank him for that. He had gotten on the phone; called people that had trucks, and told them that he wanted them there to help haul grain. If they tried to give him an excuse, he would not accept it. He told them that he expected to see their truck setting in line ready to load up.

Just before the grain trucks were ready to go, Alvin Jenkins got up on a truck and made an announcement to the crowd. Alvin told the crowd not to scratch or mess with the law enforcement people's cars. He told them that they were sent there to do a job just like we were. Then, he told the crowd that he wanted to lead them in reciting the Pledge of Allegiance. Everybody got quiet and we said the Pledge of Allegiance together. I was proud to be an American and was really touched by that gesture.

When I got in our truck, I looked at my watch and realized that it was time for the area schools to be letting out. I could just see all those buses full of kids and us with all these old farm trucks out on the road at the same time. I sure didn't want to take a chance on somebody running into a bus. So, I told Glen that I wanted to wait till 4:30 p.m. so the buses could get back to school before we left.

Glen said, "I never even thought about that, but I agree that would be a good idea."

After 4:00 p.m., we got in our trucks and got ready to go. Sandy and Paula were in the first truck ready to leave. Just then, there was a man that had changed his mind about driving his truck across the line and out of there. His wife wanted to drive the truck, but he wouldn't let her. They argued a bit about it, and then she just got out of the truck on the passenger side, came around to his side, opened the door, and dragged him out. She crawled up in the cab, locked the door, and drove the truck out herself. She just left her husband standing there, looking at her in disbelief.

We had 77 trucks and one wheelbarrow loaded with grain that crossed the line. Yes, I said wheelbarrow. There was a man that drove in from Oklahoma to help me. He loaded the wheelbarrow with grain and pushed it across the scale to have it weighed. Then, he got in line to push it off the property. He stopped to tell the FBI his name and get his picture taken as he went out.

I left a cleanup crew and told Glen that there would be some people staying to put the sheet metal back on the elevator, repaint it, grade the roads inside the complex, and pick up every piece of paper and cigarette butt they could find. Clarence Banfield, an eighty-year-old farmer from Kansas, was in charge of putting the sheet metal back on the elevator. Clarence used to work in a sheet metal shop and had ridden a bus by himself to the elevator from Kansas to help. My son, Terry, was in a car with a camera crew from Texas leading the way to the MFA Elevator at Bernie. They wanted Terry to show them how to get there so they could stop every few miles and film the convoy of trucks along the way. They had been filming the events as they happened for the past two days.

Oklahoma farmer pushes wheelbarrow loaded with grain.

Sandy drives Cryts truck to the front of the convoy.

Thousands of supporters line both sides of the road for miles.

Wayne's brother-in-law, Rick Kelly, gets a good luck kiss from Wayne's
sister, LeAnn, before heading out for Bernie with the beans.

I later saw the FBI report where Glen reported that the elevator complex was in better condition when the farmers left, than it was when they had gotten there. Even the elevator manager said if he had not seen it happen, he would swear the place had never been touched. Glen also told me that he bet George Welch that ninety-nine percent of the people who were there would cross that line. He said that one hundred percent of the people crossed the line. Even the crew that was left there to clean up came by when the last truck had left to give us their name and let us take their picture. Then, they went back to finish their job.

Farmers clean up the grounds after all the beans are loaded.

MFA Elevator at Bernie

When we arrived at the MFA Elevator in Bernie late that afternoon, it was closed. However, we had arranged to meet a licensed grain dealer at the MFA Elevator the next day to be the go-between to sell my grain. At least the worse was over for now. We decided to leave the trucks there and go home. My family and I were feeling good about getting to sell the grain and finally be able to pay off some loans. The interest rates were around eighteen percent at that time.

Hundreds of people stayed in Bernie that night, so Mayor R. B. Woods had the fire engines moved out of the stationhouse and set up some tables with coffee and cake for the farmers. He even allowed some of them to sleep in the stationhouse over night. In addition, many area businesses donated food and drink to those who had stayed to help unload the grain. Four pigs were barbecued by Paul Rink of Parma and the Chat'n Chew Restaurant catered the side dishes with enough food to feed nearly one thousand people.

Glen young and other FBI agents made a dash for a clothing store to buy fresh socks, underwear, and razors. When they had come to the Ristine Elevator, they didn't think they would be there any longer than a day or two. I think they had thought they could coerce us into giving up and going home. They didn't know how close they had come to doing so.

I remember a reporter from a radio station in Poplar Bluff named Ken Crego who had come up to me and asked if he could interview me. I told him that would be fine and he began asking me questions about events that had happened over the past couple of days and what we were going to do the next day. When the interview was over, we stood there and talked a while.

Ken told me about how he had been able to report what had happened at the Ristine Elevator before any of the other reporters. They didn't have cell phones back then, so the reporters would have to find a phone somewhere and call in their news. Ken found a farm house about a half mile north of the elevator; the next closest phone was in New Madrid. Ken said he asked the home owner Monday morning if he could use his phone to call in the story several times throughout the day. The guy told him that he could, so Ken got on the phone and called in his first report. After he was finished, he unscrewed the mouth piece in the handset and took out the microphone. He put it in his pocket and left. When other reporters asked to use the phone, it wouldn't work. The next time Ken came back to use the phone, the home owner told him that the phone was not working. Ken said he told him that he knew a little about phones and asked to look at it. Well, Ken unscrewed the mouth piece, put the microphone back in it, and called in his report. The home owner thanked him for fixing his phone and Ken went on his way. We got a chuckle about that, and soon after I left to find Sandy and the kids.

Ken Crego interviews Wayne at the Bernie MFA Elevator.

When my family and I left to go home, a couple by the name of Les and Mary Kerns from Marysville, Missouri, came home with us. We sat around the table and talked for a while. But it was difficult for me to carry on a conversation. I was so emotionally drained from the "Heat of the Battle" and the intense interrogation over the past couple of days that I felt like a worn out "dish rag." So, I excused myself and went to bed.

I was really looking forward to the next morning. I was going to be able to sell the grain and pay off my Commodity Credit loan. Then, I could start paying off some of my bills and at least begin to get back on an even keel again. I knew there were going to be legal repercussions coming as a result of what I had done, but at least I would be able to keep the "wolf away from my door" by having some money to pay off part of our bills.

We gathered up all the paperwork that we would need to sell our grain and drove back down to the MFA Elevator. We arrived sometime around 8:00 a.m. When I went in the MFA office, I saw that Glen Eaton was already there waiting for me. Glen was the licensed grain dealer that I needed to be the go-between, so I would be able to sell the grain to MFA.

We had everything ready to go. Then, I called the ASCS office at New Madrid and asked to speak to Larry Blunt. He was the director over there. I said, "Larry, this is Wayne. We are getting ready to sell the grain. I have asked that a check be issued to me every fourth load. My dad and brother are going to take the checks to the Risco Bank and cash the checks. We will be bringing you cash until there is enough to payoff the loan."

He got real quiet and then I heard him say, "Wayne, I'm sorry, but I have orders from Washington D.C., not to accept cash or check as payment for your loan."

"Larry, you can't refuse cash. You have got to accept the cash for this loan."

"Wayne, I'm sorry. You know that I would do anything I could to help you, but I have my orders. I'm telling you, I just can't do it."

Glen Young was in the office with me. I turned around and looked at him with complete astonishment. I said, "Glen, they said they won't accept cash as payment for my Commodity Credit loan."

He said, "I don't know why not. I thought they had to accept cash."

I turned around and walked out to the lobby to try to gather my thoughts. I saw Bill Anderson with his daughter Dianne there talking to each other. So, I walked over to him and said, "Bill, I just called Larry Blunt over at the ASCS office in New Madrid. I told him we were going to be bringing cash over to pay-off the loan and he said that he had orders not to accept cash or check."

Bill looked at me and said, "Wayne, you must have misunderstood. He can not refuse cash for payment of a debt."

I said, "Bill, I have been under a lot of pressure lately. I guess I could have mis-understood what he said." There was a big office in front of me with three or four desks and each one had a phone on it. I said, "Bill, let me call Larry back and make sure that I understood what he said."

I picked up the phone and looked over at Bill. He and Dianne had picked up a phone at the same time. I selected an outside line and dialed the number. They selected the same one, so they could listen to our conversation. I called the ASCS office and asked to speak to Larry Blunt again.

When he got on the phone, I said, "Larry, I'm sorry to keep bothering you. This is Wayne again. I have some reporters here with me and they are listening to our conversation. Would you care to tell them what you just told me about not accepting cash or check as payment for my loan?"

He said, "Wayne, I don't want to talk to any reporters."

I asked, "Did I hear you right? Did you just tell me that I could not pay my loan off with cash or check?"

"Wayne, I told you before that I don't understand it either, but I have orders from Washington, D.C., not to accept cash or check. I am sorry, but there is nothing I can do."

"Well, I thank you Larry."

When I hung up, Dianne said, "I've got that on tape!" She had taped our conversation. I thought that might help us put some pressure on them to change their minds. However, Bill and Dianne thought about it for a while and got worried that they might have violated the law by doing that. So, they destroyed the tape. Later, I did ask Bill and Dianne to testify at a court hearing, but Judge Baker had it stricken for the record. He said it was hearsay evidence since they were on extension phones.

I was in such a state of shock from my conversation with Larry Blunt that I don't remember how much time had passed. At that time, I decided to step outside to get some fresh air and try to clear my mind. Then, I noticed that some of the town folk had brought out a big spread of food and set it up on a table outside the office. There were several people gathered around there eating. Glen Young and other federal authorities were still in the office talking to Bill and Diane about the conversation they heard between Larry and me.

Then, I heard an auctioneer conducting an auction. When I looked around to see who it was, I saw that Frank Sifford was auctioning items that had been donated in an effort to raise money for my future legal fees. At that time, Glen stepped out the door to have a look and said, "They are auctioning off our evidence!" They had a big railroad bar, which is like a long crowbar that is angled and used to pinch the wheels on the railroad car to make the train roll. That was what they used to take the sheet metal off of the side of the elevator, so we could remove my grain. They called it the "Ristine Key." They also had a newspaper article wrapped around it that showed it being used to pry open the tin on the grain bin at the elevator. It sold for $4,000.00.

Frank Sifford auctions "Ristine Key" held by Jeff Wade.

Shortly after that, Glen and I went back inside laughing. Glen said, "Wayne, what are we going to do about your grain?"

I said, "Glen, I don't know." We sat down and thought about it for a while. Then, I said, "Glen, I'll tell you what. If I deposit this grain here in the MFA Elevator, can I get your word once again that it will remain here until we can get a determination of ownership?"

He said, "Wayne, I don't know. Judge Baker has issued a court order that says if anybody accepts any of this grain, they will be considered part of the conspiracy."

We found out earlier that morning that the Commodity Credit Corporation had threatened to pull MFA's license if they accepted the grain. The Assistant U.S. Attorney, Robert Harr also warned Bob Brown, MFA assistant district director, and Paul Carter, manager of MFA at Bernie, that the elevator could be impounded if our grain was dumped in the bins. So, the attorneys from MFA advised the elevator manager not to accept the grain.

Then, I told Glen that I had been getting calls from people in several states that offered to let me store my grain in their elevators and that they would make sure no one got it. In addition, I had a man from Florida call me and offer to pay me cash for every bushel of beans that I wanted to haul down there, but I wanted to cooperate with the FBI if there was any way possible.

Finally, I said, "Glen, you are the head of the FBI in the State of Missouri, surely you can figure out a way that we can do this."

He said, "Let me get on the phone and see what I can do."

I got up and went outside to talk to some of the people that had gathered there for the auction and waited for Glen. He was on the phone for a long time before he came outside to talk to me.

He said, "Wayne, I think we may have it in the works. I'm not going to say anymore about it until it is confirmed that we can get this done."

I said, "O.K. Glen. Thank you for your help."

By this time, the people that were there supporting me began to ask why the trucks had not been unloaded. They did not understand what was going on, but I could not tell them anything at that time. I had to wait until Glen could find out if there was anything he could do for me.

There were still thousands of people there that had been with us since Saturday and most of them needed to get back home. They had all assumed that once we got the grain removed from the Ristine Elevator and I sold my beans, it would be over. So, I had a short meeting with some of the farmers that were close to me and told them to go around and explain the situation that I was in.

While they were informing the people about what was going on, Glen came back and said, "I think we can get this pulled off, but you will have to leave the grain here once it has been deposited."

I said, "Glen, I promise that it will remain there until we have determination of ownership. If we can agree to this, I would want you to write down this agreement and I will have a notary public to notarize it. Then, I want you and George Welsh to sign it and I will sign it too."

Glen said, "All right, I will do that and then I will see if I can get my superiors to present it to the Eighth Circuit Court of Appeals in St. Louis."

We got the agreement written, signed, notarized, and on its way to St. Louis. One of their superiors was able to get the Eighth Circuit Court of Appeals in St. Louis to convene a hearing that day. After that hearing, the judge overruled Judge Baker and ordered the MFA Elevator in Bernie to take the grain. MFA was now under a court order to take the grain and it was to remain there until we had a determination of ownership. I went outside and told everybody what had happened. Everyone let out the biggest cheer when they heard that Judge Baker had been overruled.

Wayne and his brother, William Earl, celebrate unloading grain at the
Bernie MFA Elevator.

We began getting everybody in place to unload the grain. Bill Evans, an
employee of MFA, did the weighing of the trucks. He operated and electronic
scale that imprinted the information on the ticket. He also took grain samples as
the trucks were being unloaded. Another MFA employee by the name of Roger
Ray tested the samples. MFA employees, Ellsworth and Van Dine Jackson, made
the final computations to determine the net weight of the grain and completed
the MFA Weight Certificates. Then, Special Agent Gorham initialed and dated
each one. The certificates came in triplicates and MFA got one, Special Agent
Gorham got the second one, and Roger Schultz got my copy for me. There was a
little over 32,000 bushels of grain that we unloaded and stored there.

When we got home, everybody felt great about how everything turned out
that day. I felt like we had finally won the battle with help from the federal officers, Glen Young, and the Eighth Circuit Court of Appeals.

Glen and all of the federal authorities had complemented us on how everybody treated them during their presence at the Ristine Elevator and throughout
the process of getting the beans deposited. Glen could not have been more com-
plementary of the farmers, business people, and everybody that had participated
in it.

As Glen was getting ready to leave, he said, "Wayne, I would like to give you some advice. If you have anything in your name, you need to get it out as soon as possible. I don't know when an arrest warrant will be issued for you, but I can guarantee you that it will happen. When it does, how do you want to handle it?"

I asked, "Glen, what do you mean, how do I want to handle it?"

"Do you want us to come after you or do you want to give yourself up voluntarily?"

"Glen, just give me a call and I'll do whatever you want me to do."

Glen advised, "It would be better if you come in voluntarily. And I'll say it again, if you have anything in your name, you had better get it out as soon as possible. The only thing that I have seen that will stand up in court anywhere is an 'Irrevocable Trust.' No one, not a judge, a lawyer, or anybody else has ever defeated an 'Irrevocable Trust.' I would suggest that you do that for your kids. Anything that your have in your name that is free and clear with no liens against it should be put in that 'Irrevocable Trust.' The minute that it is signed and documented in the county clerk's office and they stamp it, certifying that there are no liens or judgments against it, it is irrevocable."

So, I told my family what Glen had said, and we started working on that the next day. Most of the land was in Dad's name, but we had some land in my name and my brother's and sister's names. Everything that I had was transferred out of my possession as soon as possible. Then, we met with an attorney to have the 'Irrevocable Trust' filed with the county clerk's office.

Arrest Warrant Issued

Some time later, I was speaking at a farm expo in Sikeston. Bill Anderson was there, along with other members of the media, covering the event. I was making a speech about every hour that day. Sandy was at home with the kids and got a call from Glen Young. He told her that he needed to talk to me as soon as possible. So, she drove over to Sikeston to give me the message.

"Glen Young called and they have a warrant for your arrest. He wants you to call him as soon as you can," Sandy said as she relayed the message.

I said, "O.K." and she gave me the number to call.

I went to a payphone and called the FBI office in St. Louis. I told them who I was and asked to speak to Glen Young. Glen got on the phone and asked how I was doing. I told him that I was doing fine.

Then, Glen said, "Wayne, I told you that sooner or later there would be an arrest warrant issued for you and we have it here. A complaint was filed on March 5, 1981, before U.S. Magistrate William S. Bahn charging me in violation of Title 18, Section 372, of the U.S. Code and that a warrant was issued that same day. Then, he said, "How do you want to handle it?"

"I will give myself up voluntary."

"That's good. I want you to come to our office at 1015 Locust Street in St. Louis, tell the person at the desk who you are and that you are giving yourself up, and they will notify me."

"Glen, do I need to pack a bag?"

"Pack a bag, what do you mean?"

"Will I be going to jail or what?"

"I think you will be released on your own reconnaissance."

I said, "O.K."

Glen said, "This is Thursday. Why don't you wait and come in first thing in the morning. By the time you get up here today and get processed, you may end up spending the night here in jail. Just wait until tomorrow morning."

"It would probably be around ten o'clock that morning before I could get there."

"Don't worry about it. Just get here as soon as you can tomorrow."

"OK, I'll see you there."

I left the farm expo that day and went to a law firm there in Sikeston. I told them what my problem was and that I had a warrant issued for my arrest. The attorney there said, "I know a law firm in St. Louis that is extremely good. The name of the law firm is Uthoff, Wurnson, and Graeber."

The attorney gave me the phone number and told me to contact them. So, I called and told them about my situation. They told me that they had heard about it on the news. The lawyer said, "Wayne, we will need some time to get prepared for this. Can you come up today?"

I said, "Sure, whatever we need to do."

Sandy and I went up that evening and met with the three attorneys, Uthoff, Wurnson, & Graeber to discuss my case. Kenneth Graeber took my case and explained, "This was going to be a grand jury hearing and I, as your lawyer, will not play a part in it." Mr. Graeber continued, saying, "A grand jury hearing is a prosecutor's tool in which the prosecutor presents all the evidence to the grand jury. When the prosecutor is finished, the grand jury will decide if there is enough evidence to indict you. If they do indict you, we will represent you in court. However, we do want to go with you over to the courthouse in the morning." I told them that would be fine.

The next morning, around 9:30, we met with the Mr. Graeber again. He said, "Wayne, we will take you to the Federal Marshals Office and you can turn yourself in."

I said, "No, Glen Young, who is the head of the FBI office, told me to give myself up to him."

He said, "No Wayne, that's not the way it works. I'm telling you, we don't deliver you to the FBI. I need to deliver you to the Federal Marshals Office. Trust me."

I said, "Well, that may be, but before we go over there, I want you to call the FBI headquarters and talk to Glen Young. If he says to go to the FBI office, that's what I'm going to do."

He said, "All right."

Mr. Graeber called the FBI office and told them who he was and that he was representing Wayne Cryts. Then, he asked to talk to Glen Young. Mr. Graeber said, "Sir, I am getting ready to deliver Wayne Cryts to the Federal Marshals Office." There was a pause as Glen spoke, and then Mr. Graeber said, "Oh, ohhh, ohhhhh, well O.K., that's what I'll do. We will wait here for you."

I could only hear my lawyer's side of the conversation, but I could tell by the way he was talking that Glen got a little upset with him when he said he was taking me to the Federal Marshals Office. When Mr. Graeber hung up the phone, he said, "Glen Young and another FBI agent are coming over here to meet us, and they are going to take care of you themselves. That is very unusual."

I said, "That's fine with me."

Later, Special Agents Glen Young and Homer Hoffman, Jr. came over and picked us up in their car. They took us over to the Federal Court House. I could not believe the number of press people that were there, waiting for us. You would have thought that I was a mass murderer or something. There were five or six FBI agents and several federal marshals around me as we walked toward the courthouse. When we walked up the steps, there were several photographers taking pictures and asking questions. As I opened the door and walked into the courthouse, I saw Duke Maddox, a guy that I had been friends with for years. He lived about a mile down the road from me. Duke came over, we shook hands, and stood there talking for a little while.

Then, we started down the corridor toward the elevators. A member of the camera crew got tangled up in the cords and tripped. People began falling over each other. It was like watching dominos falling one after the other. Glen Young was just shaking his head, trying to keep from laughing. He pushed the button to get an elevator. When the elevator doors opened, we walked in, and the camera crew people tried to get in there too. There were so many of them that the door would not close.

Glen said, "Hey folks, enough is enough! I want all the news media people out of here."

He took me up to the processing room and said, "Wayne, Special Agent Hoffman will take care of you now. He will fingerprint you and take your mug shot." Then, he turned to my wife and said, "Sandy, you come on down to my office and I'll entertain you until he gets finished with Wayne."

The agent and I went to the back and he tried to fingerprint me. I thought you would mash your finger on the inkpad and dab it on the paper. Agent Hoffman said, "You haven't ever done this before, have you?"

"No sir, this is my first time."

"O.K., this is how we do it. You roll your finger on the inkpad and press it down on the paper like this, then roll your finger again."

Once the fingerprinting was done, it was time for the mug shots. Agent Hoffman said, "Mr. Cryts, you will need to take your cap and jacket off, so we can get your mug shot."

I said, "All right."

I took off my denim jacket and cap, then one of the agents said, "What is that on your side?"

"Oh, that's my knife."

My lawyer started rushing in behind us and he said, "Oh! Oh! He didn't mean to bring it! He didn't mean to bbbring it!" He was stuttering all over the place.

Agent Hoffman calmly said, "Wayne, just take it off and let me have it." So, I took the knife off and gave it to him. Agent Hoffman held it up, opened the blade, and said, "My gosh, that is a big knife." Then, he folded it back up and asked my lawyer if he could catch.

He said, "Yes!" Then, the agent pitched it to him.

After the fingerprinting and mug shots were done, they took me back to Glen's office. He talked to us a little while and wanted to know how we were doing. We just sat there chit-chatting.

When we were about finished, Glen said, "The federal marshals want me to send you over to their office to fingerprint you and get a mug shot also. I'll have one of my agents go with you over there and when it is about time for court to convene, I'll come over there and walk you over to the courtroom."

So, I went over to the Federal Marshals Office and they processed me the same way the FBI did. Larry Strayhorn, the head marshal, was there along with others. When they were finished with me, Glen walked me over to the Federal Court House. I was overwhelmed by the number of people in there to see the court proceedings. They didn't allow cameras in there, but they had an artist sketching the scene. I could see her hands moving quickly and turning pages trying to capture every event as it happened.

As court began, Judge William Bahn asked me to come before the bench. I walked up there and the judge said, "Mr. Cryts, you are aware of the charges against you, and you have been read your rights."

"No Your Honor, I do not and have not."

"No Your Honor, you haven't what?"

"I'm not really sure what the charges are and I've never been read my rights."

Glen Young jumped up along with other FBI agents and federal marshals that were there and said, "Your Honor, Mr. Cryts gave himself up voluntarily and we just forgot to do that."

The judge leaned back in his chair and said, "All right, Mr. Cryts, would it be acceptable to you if I read you your rights and told you what the charges are?"

I said, "Sure, I don't have a problem with that at all, Your Honor."

So, he read me my rights and asked me if I understood them.

I said, "Yes Your Honor, I do."

Then, Judge Bahn said, "Mr. Cryts, you are charged with conspiracy to commit a crime. The maximum sentence is six years in jail and a $5,000 fine. Do you understand that?"

"Yes sir, Your Honor. I understand what that means."

The judge said, "This court sees no reason to keep you incarcerated until the grand jury makes their ruling, so I am going to release you on your own reconnaissance. The bond is set at $1,000."

"I sure appreciate that. Thank you Your Honor."

After the hearing was over, Terry Adelman, First Assistant U.S. Attorney (AUSA) in St. Louis, told me the official complaint said, "Wayne Cryts conspired with other persons to prevent the U.S. Marshals from discharging their official duties to maintain soybeans stored in the grain storage facility in Ristine, Missouri."

He also told me that AUSA Frederick Buckles had been assigned the case on February 19, 1981, and had considered several violations that he might charge me with.

After we left the courtroom, Sandy and I visited with the federal marshals and FBI agents for a while. They were embarrassed about not reading me my rights and telling me what I had been charged with. We laughed about that and the way the judge looked when I told him that I hadn't. Then, we left and went back home.

Two weeks after that hearing, I was at an AAM meeting in St. Louis. I called Sandy at home to check in with her and she said, "Wayne, your lawyer called and he wanted you to call him back when you can."

I said, "O.K. I'll give him a call."

I called my attorney and he sounded very disappointed. Mr. Graeber said, "Wayne, the grand jury met on March 18 and brought back a 'no true bill' on March 19."

I didn't know what that meant and said, "A 'no true bill'? What does that mean?"

My attorney said, "The grand jury refused to indict you, so the judge dismissed the warrant against you."

He was disappointed, because he could see the publicity that he would have had with a high profile trial. However, that was good news to me. I had been cleared by a grand jury and I felt pretty good about that.

Contempt of Court Charges Issued

Shortly after that, Judge Baker issued an order to sell all the grain at the Ristine Elevator and the grain that farmer Wayne Cryts had removed and deposited in the MFA Elevator at Bernie. In addition, Judge Baker ordered all the grain to be sold free and clear of all liens. I was astounded! I could not believe the judge had done that. I had an agreement that was signed by the federal authorities and approved by the Eighth Circuit Court of Appeals in St. Louis stating that the grain would not be sold until a determination of ownership had been made. Judge Baker totally disregarded that agreement.

Robert Lindsay, the bankruptcy trustee, sold the grain that was in the Ristine Elevator to Bearhouse, Inc. of Hamburg, Arkansas, on May 23, 1981. On June 25, 1981, he asked the MFA at Bernie to bid on my beans, but they refused. He finally sold my grain in mid-July to Bearhouse, Inc. too.

Then, Judge Baker set a date of July 13, 1981, to have the grain removed from the Ristine Elevator and sent notification to N.J. Nowell and other farmers who had grain stored there. N.J. called me at home the day that he got his notice.

He said, "Wayne, they are going to come up here and get our grain. I wish we had taken my grain out the same time you did. I don't know why we didn't; I guess we were too afraid. I really hate to ask, but would you get some of the farmers together that helped you to come over here and help us. We have got to stop them from taking our grain!"

I said, "Yes N.J., I'll do anything I can to help. I know the position that you are in."

I got a group of farmers together to be there on the day the judge had set to have the grain removed. I had a blue Ford super cab pickup and Sandy, Terry, and I drove it over there to meet N.J. and the others at the elevator. When I pulled in, I saw that George Welsh, Bob Bailey, and some other federal marshals were still there watching the elevator. I greeted them as I walked over to talk to N.J.

I told N.J., "We are going to block the entrance of the elevator."

He asked, "How are we going to do that?"

I told him that I was going to pull my pickup across half the drive and he needed to pull his Chevy Suburban across the other half of the drive. Then, we will see what happens from there. We got into our vehicles and moved them into place. I got out, raised the hood of my pickup, and stood there looking at it. N.J. and the other farmers that had come down with us gathered around my truck and started talking.

Some of the media people that were there came over and asked what was going on. I told them that my truck just took out on me. One of them asked what was wrong with it. I don't know why I said it, but I just pointed down at the engine and said, "It's got a bent dipstick." They all laughed and we continued to carry on our small talk.

Later that morning, we saw some trailer trucks coming up the highway, and, of course, we had the entrance blocked. When they saw us, they pulled off on the shoulder of the road.

George Welsh went out, got on the running board of one of the trucks, and told the lead driver who he was and what he was doing there. He told the driver, "The entrance is blocked, and if I were you, I would turn these trucks around and head back to Arkansas."

When George told them that, they decided that was all they needed to hear. So, they pulled around to the front of the elevator to turn around and headed home. We were feeling good that we had stopped them again. N.J. thanked us for our help.

That night, when we got home, the phone rang and it was a reporter. Doyle Patton, from Little Rock, called to talk to me. He said, "Wayne, what in the world did you do up there today?"

I said, "Judge Baker had sent some trucks up here to load the grain and we turned them around."

"Do you know what they are running on television and radio stations down here?"

"No, I don't have any idea."

"They are saying that Judge Baker's efforts to remove the Ristine grain were thwarted by a 'bent dipstick'."

When I heard that, I just laughed and laughed about that. But, I didn't think too much else about it and we continued to talk about what had happened that day.

I found out later that Judge Baker had issued "Contempt of Court" charges against me and a "John Doe" for blocking the entrance to the elevator. The federal marshals had taken pictures of us the day that we blocked the drive, but since they had taken pictures of us every time we had been there, we didn't think much about it. My son, Terry, was with me that day and they had a picture of him sitting in the back of the truck. We found out later that he was the "John Doe" that the judge had issued charges against who was with me that day. However, we were able to get those charges dropped when the judge found out he was only fourteen years old.

Judge Baker also charged N.J. Nowell, Robert Henry, John Henry, Cecil Beeson, and Joe Broughton that were there to help block the entrance to the elevator with "Contempt of Court." Some of those people were named specifically and others were listed as "John Does" if the marshals did not know their names.

When Judge Baker issued "Contempt of Court" charges against us with fines of $3,000 each, it really scared the other farmers. So, they hired a lawyer to represent them and I had decided not to be part of that. Their lawyer talked to Judge Baker to find out how they could get the charges dropped. I believe Judge Baker told their lawyer that if the farmers would stop their fight and let him remove the grain, he would drop the charges. They all agreed to do so. When the judge dropped the charges against those farmers, he dropped the charges against me also. So, I no longer had any charges issued against me.

Then, Judge Baker held a news conference and informed the news media that he would be removing all the grain from the Ristine Elevator, and then they were going to the Bernie MFA Elevator to remove Wayne Cryts' grain. Up until that point, I had no intentions of going back to the MFA Elevator until a determination of ownership had been made about the grain, because I had an agreement with the FBI that was affirmed by the Eighth Circuit Court of Appeals in St. Louis.

I did not think I could go through that type of pressure again. So, I tried to put together several contingency plans to deal with this situation. I didn't know if he would send someone up in trucks or on a train. One idea I had was to lie down in front of the trucks or on the train tracks, so they could not move. I was determined not to let them take my grain.

Then, I remembered that Ralph Mouser, our Stoddard County Sheriff, had been very supportive during my last ordeal. Then, I thought to myself, "If they are coming up here to take my private property, then they would be stealing my grain."

So, I went to see Ralph at his home in Dexter and I planned to ask him if he would arrest them. When I got down there, Ralph came outside to talk to me. I told him that I needed a big favor. He asked me what it was and I told him that

Judge Baker would be sending some trucks up here to take my grain out of the MFA Elevator in Bernie. I reminded him that I was a taxpayer here in Stoddard County and that I wanted him to arrest the truck drivers, warehouse officials, federal marshals, and anyone else that tried to steal my grain.

Ralph looked at me and said, "Aw Wayne, I can't do that. Do you know what would happen to me if I arrested a federal marshal?"

I said, "Ralph, I'm asking for your help. You are supposed to uphold the law and protect the citizens of this county. They are getting ready to steal my grain. I have documented warehouse receipts for every bushel of grain to prove that it is my private property, and I want it protected."

He stood there for a minute, thinking, and said, "Wayne, get in the car with me and let's go to the jail."

When we got there, he started dragging down books and looking through them. Finally, he stopped and said, "Right here, Wayne, under Missouri Law Chapter 544, Section 180, it says that if a citizen of Missouri sees what they believe to be a felony being committed, then you as a citizen, have the right to arrest that person or persons and take them to jail." Ralph then added, "If you want to arrest them and bring them to jail, then I will hold them for at least twenty-four hours."

I said, "Good enough, that's my plan. I will do it." I called several of my supporters, told them what my plan was, and asked them to help me. They told me that they would be there.

Then, I got a letter from the Commodity Credit Corporation informing me that they were calling my loan and if I was unable to pay off my loan, then I would forfeit my grain. That really infuriated me, because I had already tried to pay them with a check and in cash. But, they refused the money under orders from Washington. I was at the point now that I did not have the assets to pay off the loan. However, the letter also said I could pay off my loan with the commodity itself. When I finished reading that letter, I decided to change my plans and informed the others.

My first thought was to take enough grain up there to the ASCS office, stick an auger through the window of the office, and start unloading the grain. Then, tell them to holler when they felt like they had enough grain to pay off the loan. However, I learned a long time ago, never to make a decision in anger. When I calmed down, I remembered that the people who worked in that office were my friends and that it was not their fault. They were just doing their jobs.

Finally, I decided that I was going to have to go back to the elevator in Bernie and remove my grain. I called a bunch of my supporters again, told them what I was going to do, and asked them for their help. They asked me when I planned to do it. I told them that I had not set a date yet, but I would let them know when I had the details worked out. Then, I called Eric Thompson, the manager of MFA, and told him that I was going to remove my grain from the elevator. He said, "Wayne, we've been expecting it ever since we heard that the judge had announced he was going to take your grain. We really have a problem. It's going to jeopardize MFA, if we assist you."

I said, "Eric, I want to apologize to you. I know that you did not volunteer to be a part of this. I won't do it, if it's going to jeopardize MFA."

Eric said, "I've already talked to our lawyer about this and he told me that the only way you can do it and keep us in the clear is to let it be known that you are prepared to use force if necessary. Wayne, you know what that's going to do to you."

I said, "Yes, I do. We have become friends in a short period time and I want to apologize to you again."

Eric told me not to worry about it. He said, "If you want to make the announcement that you are prepared to use force if necessary, the company will allow you to take your grain. And, if you do decide to remove your grain, you will need to go down there by yourself sometime and talk to the supervisor. Just tell him that you are there to see how the operation is run."

The next day, I went down there to see the manager and he took me to the area where the grain was loaded and unloaded. I saw a big spout up there and he took me over to the wall and showed me two buttons there.

He said, "Do you see that top button, if someone were to push that one, the grain would start pouring out of that spout. If someone were to push the bottom one, it would stop the grain."

Then, he told me there was nothing in that area except the grain that I had brought in for storage. I told him thanks and left.

I called Eric Newhouse, who was an Associated Press reporter, and told him that I needed a favor. I asked him if he would meet me at the MFA Elevator in Bernie the next day, which was July 22. I needed him to be there when I went into the MFA office to inform them that I was there to get my grain and that I was prepared to use force if necessary. I let him know that I needed to make that statement in order to protect the MFA elevator from any charges being brought against them. Sometimes the media can be your best defense.

When I got down there the next morning, there were already trucks lined up and ready to load. I walked into the office and the reporter was there when I met with Paul Carter, supervisor, and told him that I was there to get my grain and that I was prepared to use force if necessary. Paul told me that he did not want any of his employees to be harmed, so they would not get in my way.

We were already loading grain by the time Federal Marshals Bailey and Welsh came over from the Ristine Elevator. George Welsh came over to me and said, "Well, we got a phone call informing us that the grain was being moved out of the Bernie Elevator. So, we came over to verify it."

I told him that I didn't have any other choice and he told me good luck. Then, they got in their car and drove off.

Evans Ipock, Bill Jewell, and John Clampet were the ones operating the buttons loading the grain on the trucks as they went through. When we got the grain loaded, I took the grain to the ASCS office in Bloomfield. We had grain that had been harvested in both Stoddard County and New Madrid County. We had warehouse receipts for all the grain that had been deposited. I announced to the news media that I was taking the grain to the ASCS office in Bloomfield, so they would know that I was coming. George Putman was the director of the ASCS office at that time. A friend of ours, Vera Almond of Aid, also worked there. When I walked in the office, she gave me a big hug.

Mr. Putman was there waiting for me and I said, "Mr. Putman, I have a letter stating that you have called my loan. It also states right here in the letter that I can pay off my loan with the commodity itself. I realize that you do not have the facilities to handle this grain, so you can designate any elevator you want, and I will deliver it there. I will haul enough grain to the elevator of your choice to satisfy the loan."

Mr. Putman said, "Wayne, I have been told not to accept the grain."

I was very frustrated at that time, because the letter clearly stated that I could pay off my loan with the commodity itself.

I took a deep breath and said, "George, I'm not blaming you. I just don't know what they want. I tried to pay off my loan with a check and was refused. Then, I tried to pay it with cash and was refused. Now, I was sent a letter that clearly stated that I could pay the loan off with the commodity itself, and now you are telling me that you will not accept my grain as payment. I have made every effort to pay off my debt. You can call me when they decide what they want. Until that time, I plan to sell this grain if I can. Then, I am going to start paying some of my bills."

Mr. Putnam said, "Wayne, I hope you understand that I would accept your grain if I could, but I am under orders not to do so."

I told George, "I understood that. When you find out what your superiors want done about my loan, then call me."

He said, "All right."

When we left the office, I had made up my mind that I did not want the trustee and bankruptcy lawyers to get my grain. I knew that I would not get a penny from the grain after they got paid their fees for the bankruptcy proceedings. So, I told all the farmers who were there that had helped me through all this to take the grain and sell it wherever they could.

Dispersement of Grain

As I stood there looking at all the trucks full of grain, I realized that I was finally to the point that if I never got a dime of the money for the grain, I didn't care any more. I decided to make an announcement to the farmers about the grain they had in the trucks.

"Judge Baker has reissued his order again that if any elevators take any of this grain, they will be considered part of the conspiracy. The James Brothers headquarters is located in Corning, Arkansas, and Judge Charles Baker is in charge of those elevators too. The only thing I'm asking someone to do is deliver at least two truck loads of grain to the elevator in Corning, and I want that ticket and receipt."

Harley Sentel said, "I guarantee there will be at least two loads that will go to that elevator."

I said, "That's what I've got to have to protect the other elevators. If he comes down on other elevators because they took part of my grain, then all I have to do is walk into his court with those receipts and ask him if he is part of the conspiracy also?"

We drove our trucks on home and unloaded the grain in a barn at our house and stored it there until we were able to market it later. Then, I went about my business as usual. Every once in a while, I would get a call from a farmer who would say, "Wayne, I have something for you, why don't you come by." I would go by and find out that they had sold the grain, cashed the check, and put the money in brown paper bags.

Here I was, selling nearly 30,000 bushels of beans and picking up the money in paper bags. I didn't know what to do with that much cash. If people found out that I had a lot of cash in the house, I was afraid that I might be robbed. So, I had some friends of mine, Bob and Joyce Hardin to go rent a couple of safety deposit boxes in the bank at Risco, so I could keep the cash in it. Then, I had to figure out what to do with all that cash.

I called my CPA, Ed Barry at Sikeston, and said, "Ed, this is Wayne. I have a little bit of a problem."

He just laughed and said, "You got a little problem? What have you got going on?"

I said, "Well, I'm beginning to accumulate some cash."

"Oh Wayne" he said. "The IRS is going to eat you alive!"

I said, "I thought I was paying a good CPA to keep me out of tax problems."

Ed said, "What are you doing?"

I said, "It seems like the farmers just scattered with my grain when they left the Bernie Elevator. They have been selling it, cashing the checks, and I'm picking it up in brown paper bags. Right now, I've got it in safety deposit boxes, but I need to pay some bills. I need you to tell me how to do that."

He said, "Let me sleep on this and try to come up with something we can do. Call me tomorrow."

I called Ed the next day and he said, "Wayne, first off, the IRS doesn't care where you get your money." He jokingly said, "They don't care if you rob banks, just as long as they get their part of it. You have got to document that cash with money orders when you pay your bills. That way, you will have a paper trail to document the cash that you have. If you do that, you will be all right."

I said, "That's what I will do."

We were finally able to start paying our bills, but ran out of money before I could pay them all.

By this time, my income taxes were also due. So, I filed my taxes on time like I was supposed to. However, I didn't send any money with it, because I just didn't have it. As you can imagine, the IRS began sending nasty letters to me demanding payment of my taxes. Then, they ordered me to come to St. Louis to meet with them at their office. So, I called my brother-in-law, Henry Cookson, because he knew the town very well and how to get to the IRS office. I walked in the IRS office and introduced myself. I told this lady that I was having a little problem getting my taxes paid.

She got my file and said, "Yes Mr. Cryts, I can see that." Then, she told me how much I owed and asked me if I was prepared to pay it?

I said, "Yes ma'am, I am. The problem is I don't have any money."

She said, "You don't have any money, but you are prepared to pay your taxes?"

I said, "Yes ma'am. The IRS confiscates things at times to get their money don't they?"

She said, "Yes."

I told her, "I don't have any money, but I have some soybeans and I could haul enough soybeans to a place that you designate and you could seize them to pay my IRS bill."

She said, "Well, that could probably be done. Let me get my supervisor and see what she says."

She came back with her supervisor and I went through the same story for her. The supervisor said, "Well, this is highly unusual, but I think we can do that. Just a minute, our district supervisor happens to be here today. Let me ask him."

He came out and I explained the whole thing to him. All of a sudden, he straightened up in his chair and said, "You're that soybean Cryts person aren't you?"

I said, "Yes sir. I'm probably the one you are referring to."

He said, "You're not getting us in the middle of that mess!"

Then, he said, "Mr. Cryts, do you intend to pay this bill?"

I said, "Yes sir. As soon as I can get some money, I will pay my taxes."

He said, "All right. If that is what you are intending to do, then you won't have any more problems with us. I can understand what you must be going through. When you get to where you can pay your taxes, then send us the money."

From that time on, they never sent me another letter or called asking me to pay them. They were as nice to me as they could possibly be. When I was able to get enough money to pay my taxes, I sent it to them.

I have always wondered what would have happened if they had taken the grain. I would like to have seen a battle between a federal judge and the IRS to see who was the meanest. It would have been really interesting to see how that battle would end up. I would have enjoyed informing Judge Baker that I didn't know where all the grain went, but I know who had part of it.

Removal of Grain from Cargill Elevators

In 1981, along with fighting all the legal battles, I helped on the farm all I could to harvest the 1981 crop. It was probably some of the toughest times we ever went through because not only did we have the pressure of all the court proceedings, but I was constantly worried about being arrested and hauled off to jail. Our cash flow was near zero by this time as well, and Judge Baker had issued an order to over a hundred banks in our area to confiscate any money that we had deposited with them.

During this time, we often received help from people all over the area. Sandy told me that two women from Memphis, Missouri, had driven down to the house one day with a pickup load of chemicals in it for us to be able to spray our fields. Sandy said the ladies told her that they figured we could use it and that their husbands wanted to help us for taking a stand against an unjust law. As we struggled that fall to get the crop in, friends offered to help.

Carlos Welty, a good friend of mine who was also at the elevator with me called and said, "Wayne, I'm going to bring my combine over and help you harvest your crop."

I said, "Carlos, you have already done so much for me. I really do appreciate it."

Carlos used his own equipment and fuel. He knew that I didn't have any money to pay him with.

As we harvested the crops, I thought that as soon as I sold this year's grain, some of my money problems would be lessened. But, it was not to be. We were over at New Madrid on a farm we had back in the bottoms and we combined for about three days. We only had a little over 3000 bushels of grain harvested when it started raining. Sandy had been hauling the grain over to the Cargill Elevators in New Madrid to deposit it. She had gotten scale tickets for each load that she took over there. This was my first opportunity, since the battle had started back in August of 1980, to have a chance to sell some grain and get some cash flow going again.

Since it was raining, I decided to go to the Cargill Elevators at New Madrid and tell them I would like to collect on the grain that I had brought in. The manager said, "Wayne, I'm really sorry about this, but we have a court order from Judge Baker to hold that grain here until they can confiscate it. I am really sorry, but there is nothing I can do about it."

I was not prepared to hear that. I was devastated once again. Here I thought I was going to get some cash flow going, so I could pay off some of those high interest rate loans. The interest rates had jumped from seven percent to twenty percent. We had a lot of debt and I was counting on that crop to help us get over the hump.

I stood there for a few minutes trying to gather my thoughts. Then, I said, "I'm going to have to have the grain or a check."

He said, "Wayne, we get our orders out of our headquarters in Sikeston and you will have to talk to somebody there."

When I got home that night, I called Carlos and told him what had happened. I told him that I was going to Sikeston in the morning to talk to someone at Cargill headquarters about getting this resolved.

He said, "I want to go with you if that is O.K."

I said, "That would be fine with me."

The next morning, Carlos came to our house; we got in my pickup and started that way. Carlos is the farmer that I refer to as never having a "reverse." He believes in tackling a problem head on and if it doesn't move, then he will go through or over it.

On the way over to Sikeston, I said, "Carlos, when we get over there, let's be nice and polite until we find out exactly what's going on and where we are at."

I'll never forget that look on Carlos' face as he turned and said, "Do you want to be nice and polite before we wipe the floor with the SOB's or after."

I said, "Let's just wait and see where we are at."

When we got here, we went into the headquarters and I told them who I was and what I wanted to discuss. The manager came out and introduced himself. Then he said, "We really apologize for this, Mr. Cryts, and sympathize with what has happened to you. I can't imagine what you must be going through, but there is nothing we can do. We have a court order from Judge Baker and we can't do anything about it."

I said, "I understand your position and where you are at, but I have got to have my grain. I'm just as serious as I can be. I want my money or my grain."

"Mr. Cryts, there is nothing we can do."

"Those elevators are all concrete and its going to be tough busting in one of them sir. I don't know right now how I'm going to do it, but I will remove my grain from the elevator. I'll do the least amount of damage that I can, and I will pay to get it repaired after I'm done."

Then, the manager said, "Wayne, our head office in Minnesota is not open yet. Would you mind waiting until I can talk to them and see if we can't get something worked out?"

"Sure. I think that would be a good idea."

Carlos and I sat down in the manager's office and he brought us some coffee. We talked until it was time for him to call the head office. Then, he asked if we would mind going out into the lobby while he made his call.

I said, "Not at all" and we went out to the lobby.

He was on the phone for quite some time. When he came out of his office, he said, "Wayne, I'm sorry. There is really nothing we can do."

I said, "I appreciate your trying to help. I am going to go get my trucks and some people to help me, and then I will be back to get my grain. I have got to have that grain."

He said, "Well, let me call them back and make sure they completely understand the situation."

He went back to his office, called them back, and had another conversation with them. When he finished, he came back out and told me that they wanted to wait until they could contact their attorneys to find out if there was anything else they could do. We sat around there for over three hours waiting for them to tell us something.

Finally, sometime after 11:00 that morning, the manager asked us to come back in his office and said, "The president of the company has had a meeting with the lawyers and they advised him that there was nothing that could be done about the court order. However, the president of the company told me to let you have your grain. The problem we have now is that New Madrid is a barge facility. We do not have a load out facility for trucks there."

I hadn't even thought about that, but that was a major problem for us. Then, the manager said, "We have seven inland elevators that you can choose from to get your grain. Which one would be the most convenient for you?"

"The one at Dexter would work out better for me."

"That will be fine. You get your trucks, take them over there, and I will call them and have all the paperwork ready for you when you get there. Then, we will load up the exact amount of grain from that elevator that you put in at New Madrid."

I thanked him for his cooperation and told him that I was sorry that I had put them in that situation.

He said, "I can't understand, but I can imagine what you are going through."

It was still wet up in the bottoms where all of our trucks were located, which was two miles back up in a field. So, I called Homer Evans at the AAM office in Puxico. I asked him to get in touch with my brother and my dad and have them to meet me at the farm in New Madrid, because we had to get the trucks out to the highway. It was still raining and I figured we would have to hook on to them with tractors and drag them out of there. Carlos and I left and went over to the farm to get started. By the time we got the trucks drug out to the highway, my dad and William Earl had arrived. Then, we drove the trucks to the Cargill facility in Dexter. When we pulled in, there were trucks already lined up and loaded with our grain. We didn't even have to use our trucks.

When I got out and walked over to see what was going on, I saw that Quincy Murphy was there. Quincy was the one who could get the trucks when you needed them. He was the guy who helped me get the trucks I needed the last two times I had to remove my grain from storage. The farmers were sitting around there waiting for me to tell them what to do with the grain.

I told them, "I have got to sell this grain, because I need the money. Let's try the MFA storage facility at Bernie. If they won't take it, then we will go from one elevator to another until we find one that will buy the grain."

So, we got in our trucks and headed to Bernie. When I walked in to the MFA facility, they knew who I was and what was going on.

I said, "I've got some grain I would like to sell if you can help me."

They looked at each other and said, "That's what we are in the business for."

They told me that they didn't have a court order against it. I was relieved to hear that, because that was the first good news I had heard in a long time. So, we pulled our trucks in there and unloaded them. As soon as we were done, they wrote me a check.

I laughed and told everybody, "This is the third time that I have loaded grain out of an elevator. I think I'm getting better at taking it out than I am at putting it in!"

Everybody busted out laughing when they heard that. Then, I thanked them for their help and we all went home. That was the last time, the judge tried to confiscate my grain or prevent me from selling it.

However, this battle went on and on. Every time we got to a point where we thought it was over, they would serve more papers on us. For a while, we dreaded going to the mailbox or answering the phone. We never knew if it was going to be a federal marshal informing us that they had papers to serve on me or the post office letting me know that they have a certified letter for me.

Certified letters meant that it was a court order from the judge and I would think, "What now?" I remember waking up at night with my stomach tied up in knots after I received a court order from Judge Baker notifying me to appear in court. I knew that I didn't have a chance in his court and that I was totally at his mercy. However, my family, friends and farmers from around the country never gave up on me.

Court in Little Rock

Sandy and I were ordered by Judge Baker to come to Little Rock to appear before his court on February 09, 1982. We went down there the day before we were scheduled to be in court. Many of our friends and farmers from the area went down with us to be at this hearing. One thing that concerned me most about this court hearing was the possibility of going to jail.

At this point in time, we did not have any money left to pay an attorney. Judge Baker had had us in and out of court hearings for months and many times he would cancel the hearing the day we got there. I was told about a group in Klamath Falls, Oregon, that specialized in constitutional law. The group's name was American Constitutional Rights Association and Perry Chestnut was the executive director. A representative from the group had called and told me that their lawyers would take my case for free. However, Judge Baker refused to recognize them in court. So, we borrowed some money to hire a lawyer, Basil Hicks of Little Rock, that the judge would recognize and the lawyers from Oregon worked through him.

The farmers that had come along with us told me that they were not going to let the judge put me in jail.

I said, "Now look, this thing has been peaceful up to now and I don't want any violence. Whatever happens, we will deal with it. You have to stay under control."

Harley Sentel from Qulin looked at me and said, "Wayne, if they put you in jail, then that's O.K. If that is what you want, we will remain cool, calm, and collected. But, I'm telling you right now, if they put Sandy in jail, we are not going to remain calm. We will not stand by and let the judge put her in jail."

I said, "Harley, that goes for Sandy too."

He said, "Wayne, we have listened to you all the way through this ordeal, but he is not going to put Sandy in jail."

I said, "I'm telling you, that's the way I want it."

He said, "Well, we will see how everything develops."

That worried me, because that was the first time any of the farmers told me that they may not listen to me.

The next day, we went over to the courtroom and Judge Baker convened court. Sandy was not allowed to be in the courtroom with me, because they did not want her to hear my testimony. I had Tom Kershaw, Perry Chestnut, Fred Brown of Klamath Falls, Oregon, and Basil Hicks of Little Rock as my lawyers working on the case. Jack Lassiter and F. Lee Bailey joined the case later when my legal defense fund was established.

When my lawyers and I walked in, I saw six bankruptcy lawyers sitting together on the front row. In addition, there were a lot of spectators and reporters there to see what would happen at this hearing. Then, Judge Baker walked in and everyone stood up until he sat down. At that time, I was ordered to come up to the stand and be sworn in.

The bankruptcy lawyers began to ask me questions about what happened the day I removed my grain from the Ristine Elevator. They began by asking me if I removed the grain out of the elevator and I said, "Yes, I did."

Then, they asked me questions about what went on that day and I answered those questions too. Then, one of the lawyers asked me to name the farmers that helped me remove the grain that day and I told him that I could not do that. He just kept asking that same question and I kept giving him the same answer.

Finally, Judge Baker said, "Mr. Cryts, you are instructed to answer the question. You will name the people that helped you to remove the grain from the elevator."

The lawyer asked me once again who helped me remove the grain from the elevator? I said, "I can not answer that question and I will not answer that question."

Finally, the judge instructed my lawyers to take me outside and explain to me that if I didn't answer the question as instructed, he would find me in "contempt of court" and that I would be incarcerated until I answered the question.

Once we were outside the courtroom, my lawyer explained to me that "contempt of court" means "you are in jail with the keys in your pocket." He explained that I was not being put in jail for punishment, but to coerce me to purge myself of "contempt of court." Anytime that I was ready to comply with the court order, all I had to do was notify the authorities. Then, I would be released from jail to come back to court and answer the question.

My lawyers went over this several times with me and then asked if I understood what they were telling me? I told them that I did understand what would happen if I refused to answer the question.

My lawyers told me one more time, "If you don't answer the question, you will go to jail. And if you remain stubborn, you could very likely be there for a long time, because we don't see the judge relenting on this. Do you understand that?"

I said, "Yes, I do."

Then, my lawyer asked, "Are you going to answer the court's question?"

I said, "No I'm not. I cannot in good conscience tell them who helped me. Besides, they already know who was there that day, because the FBI took a picture of everyone and wrote their names down as well. I don't understand why they are asking me questions that they already have the answer to."

My lawyer said, "That may be, but the judge is demanding that you personally name them."

I said, "I don't know the proper words to use, but I'm going to take the Fifth Amendment."

"I don't know if the judge will let you take the Fifth Amendment."

"What do you mean? I thought I had a right to take the Fifth Amendment."

"It is the judge's decision as to whether he allows you to do that."

I said, "All right."

We went back in the courtroom and Judge Baker ordered me back to the witness stand.

He said, "Mr. Cryts, have your lawyers informed you of the penalties for not answering the question as instructed and what may very well happen to you?"

I said, "Yes Your Honor, they have."

He said, "I am ordering you to name the farmers that helped you remove the grain."

I said, "Your Honor, I don't know the proper words that I'm supposed to use, but I want to take the Fifth Amendment."

Judge Baker had a pencil in his hand at that moment and he got so mad that he threw the pencil across the courtroom. Then, he looked at me and said, "Mr. Cryts, I'm going to ask you again, who helped you remove your grain?"

I said, "Your Honor, I plead the Fifth Amendment."

He then turned to the bankruptcy lawyers and told them to ask me the question again, so they began asking me the same question over and over and over. I continued to give them the same answer as well.

After this had gone on for a while, I finally looked up at the judge and said, "Your Honor, I mean no disrespect for this court, but I am so sick and tired of this forced mockery of justice and those thieving, money hungry lawyers that come in to a bankrupt elevator like a bunch of vultures and milk every dollar out of the escrow account. And by the time they are finished, the farmers are left with nothing. They take the assets of honest hard-working people and get rich off them." Then, after a pause, I added, "Your Honor, I think this circus has gone on long enough. You do whatever you have to do and let's get on with it."

It was so quiet in there you could hear a pin drop. Everybody was just setting there waiting for Judge Baker's reaction. I didn't know what he was going to do either.

Finally, Judge Baker said, "I agree, this circus has gone on long enough. I'm going to recess this court until I can get a ruling from the Attorney General as to whether you can take the Fifth Amendment or not." Then, he banged the gavel, got up, and out he went.

About two weeks later, I was notified that they were going to reconvene court and I was ordered back to Little Rock. Again, Sandy wasn't allowed in the court room. Judge Baker ordered me back on the witness stand.

Then, he said, "Mr. Cryts, you have been granted immunity to prosecution. If you will answer this court's question, you will be free to go because we cannot use anything you say against you. In doing so, that waives your Fifth Amendment right. Therefore, you do not need the Fifth Amendment to protect you. Do you understand that?"

I said, "Yes, Your Honor; I understand."

He said, "All right. I am ordering you to start naming the farmers that helped you."

I set there for a little bit thinking about what I was going to do, then I looked up and said, "Your Honor; I can not in good conscience…", and that's as far as I got.

The judge turned to the federal marshal and said, "Mr. White, you will take Mr. Cryts into custody. You will incarcerate him and he will remain there until he purges himself of contempt of court."

The marshal led me out of the courtroom and put me in the holding cell. My son, Terry, made his way down to the holding area where I was being held, but the guard stopped him before he could get to me. The guard told him that if he did not leave he would arrest him. Terry told the guard that he was my son, but the guard did not believe him at first. Terry kept coming toward me and I told the guard that he was my son. Terry was very upset that I had been put in jail.

Sandy told me later that Paula kept asking her why the judge put her daddy in jail, because he was not the one that did anything wrong. Paula said, "Daddy is not the criminal. The James Brothers were the ones that lied, saying all the grain in the elevators was theirs, which caused all this anyway."

Later, court was reconvened and Sandy was put on the witness stand. The bankruptcy lawyer started asking her questions about what happened the day we removed our grain from the Ristine Elevator. Sandy told me that they asked her about forty questions that day including who helped us. She said she gave them her name and whatever personal information they asked for. And then, simply took the Fifth Amendment. When they realized she was not going to answer any questions, they dismissed her.

I was transferred to the Pope County Jail in Russellville, Arkansas, on April 28, 1982, and processed in there. The county jail houses federal prisoners under a contract with the U.S. District Court in Little Rock. When they were finished, I was put in a cell and I spent the rest of the night there. The next morning, I got up early, took a shower, and got cleaned up. Shortly after that they brought breakfast around to everyone.

F. Lee Bailey, who had joined my legal team at this time, filed a motion with the judge requesting that I be released temporarily until a motion could be filed to request bail. Judge Baker denied the motion with a ten-page ruling stating, "Cryts can be released from jail by telling the truth, the whole truth and nothing but the truth." Then, he said, "Cryts has planted the seeds of sedition and must harvest the bittersweet bounty of his own folly by staying in jail."

A couple of days after I had been in jail there, Sheriff Jim Bolin came back and said, "Wayne, we are being bombarded with phone calls. They are calling from literally all over the nation and totally tying up our switchboards. I don't know what to do about it. Do you want to answer these phones calls?"

"Yes, if it's permissible, I would sure like to do that."

"It can be arranged."

They had a small conference room in the jail and the sheriff decided to set things up in there for me. They set up a table and brought in a telephone that had seven outside lines on it.

Each morning, I would get up, take a shower, eat breakfast, and go to the conference room around 6:30 a.m. and did not finish until about 9:00 that night. By the time I got to the conference room each morning, every light on the phone would already be lit up. I would punch the top button, talk to whoever was on there, and work my way down. When I finished with the bottom line, I would go to the top and start over again. I had calls from farmers giving me support, telling me to hang in there, and that they were praying for me. In addition, there were numerous newspaper, radio, and television reporters wanting to interview me. This helped get the information out to the American people about the problems the farmers had with grain elevators that went through bankruptcy. I did that day after day the whole time I was in jail there. Eventually, one of the jailers went out, got me a nameplate, and put it on my desk.

Some of the people from Russellville also came over to meet with me in the conference room. I found them to be very nice people that wanted to know first hand what I had been through and why I was in jail there. The second night that I was in jail, I remember that an elderly man came in to see me. He had three bananas and two apples that he had bought from a local grocery store that he gave me. We talked for a while about what my family and I had been through over the past couple of years and he left with tears in his eyes. It is hard to express how I felt when this happened, but I was proud to know that people from all over the country supported my cause.

Family meets with Wayne at Pope County Detention Center on week-
ends.

Sandy stayed at the Holiday Inn Hotel in Little Rock while I was in jail there in Russellville. She told me that the hotel manager told her the bill had been taken care of and that it would not cost her anything when she stayed there. Paula stayed with Robert and Pearl Eck during the week while she went to school. My sister, LeAnn, and her husband, Rick Kelley, stayed with Terry on the farm and kept it going for us. Family members brought the kids down every Friday to the jail to visit Sandy and me for the weekend. Sandy said the Eck's would give her money to help with the expenses.

Schools in the area also got permission to bring some of their classes over to visit with me. The Russellville High School current events class taught by Mr. John Eitenmiller came to the jail. I began by telling them about the elevator situation and informed them as to why I was in jail there at that time. Then, I told them that the silent majority in this country is going to have to become vocal and more active in our government. Many of us have taken this country for granted to long. I also told them that I was very proud of the fact that there have been thousands of people involved in the protest and no one has been hurt. I finished by telling them that if the world is not in better condition when you leave it than when you arrived, then you have failed in life.

Wayne speaks to area students in Pope County Detention Center conference room.

I had received so much positive press from people in the area that the Mayor of Russellville, Ron Russell, came over and presented me the key to the city. The mayor told me, "This key will literally get me into anything in Russellville."

I said, "Mr. Mayor, I am deeply honored and really appreciate that, but I really wish I had a key to get me out of something in Russellville!" We all had a big laugh over that one.

Many of my friends and supporters started a peaceful protest outside the courtroom in Little Rock and the Pope County Jail in Russellville. Several people drove tractors in with yellow ribbons on them as a sign of support. One group of farmers drove their tractors down from Michigan. There were people there from many states to show support. I would always tell them that their support was my strength.

When I went back to my cell at night, I would have to go down a hallway until I reached a door with iron bars across it. I would go through the door to my cell, which was the first one on the left. I remember one evening that I didn't get to bed until around 1:00 a.m. in the morning. Then, I heard what sounded like an army marching down the hallway. The door was slammed opened and some officers came in my cell. It was Sheriff Bolin, some deputies, and some state troopers. They came over, pulled me up out of my bed, and literally dragged me down to the conference room. There was a big spotlight set up in there and they sat me down in a chair in front of it.

One of them said, "Mr. Cryts, you are in very serious trouble!"

I was absolutely bewildered, because we had gotten along so good to that point. However, I could tell by looking at the expression on their faces that they were determined to do something and I was setting there trying to figure out what in the world was going on.

The sheriff was doing most of the questioning and he said, "Mr. Cryts, where were you at approximately 10:00 p.m. last night?"

I said, "I think I had already gone back to my cell."

He said, "Now Mr. Cryts, we know better than that!"

They just kept asking me about where I was and what I had been doing last night.

I finally said, "What is going on?"

The sheriff said, "I want you to look at this report Mr. Cryts."

I took the report and started reading it. The report stated that somebody had broken into a farmer's grain bin the previous night around 10:30 p.m. and stole some soybeans.

The sheriff said, "We know this has got to be you!"

None of them cracked a smile or anything. I looked up and swore that I had not left the jail. Then, they just busted out laughing. They laughed so hard that tears came to their eyes. Those guys really had me fooled and I will never forget that. We had a big laugh out of that. The deputies and I got along so well that they even pitched in money to help with my expenses.

The state troopers from that area hung out in the conference room when they took their breaks, so I got to know them pretty well. We would set around, drink coffee, and talk. Of course, they would tell their war stories about different things that had happened to them and I would tell them mine.

Sheriff Bolin came in one morning and asked, "Wayne, do you know Bill Clinton?"

I said, "Yes, he is the Governor of Arkansas."

He said, "He was the Governor of Arkansas and he is now running for governor again. He wants to meet with you and asked if it would be alright?"

I said, "Sure, I would be glad to meet with him."

So, Bill Clinton came in and we met in the conference room. We had a real good discussion about what I had been through. He was very concerned about me and asked if I was being treated well.

Bill Clinton meets with Wayne in the Pope County Detention Center.

I said, "I have heard of Southern hospitality and I've been treated very well here by everyone here in Arkansas except a judge and some bankruptcy lawyers."

Bill Clinton said, "Mr. Cryts I understand what you are doing and why you are doing it. I commend you for your stand and for the way you have conducted yourself. This thing has grown into a big political issue and is gaining momentum across the country. There are a lot of politicians beginning to get involved in it."

Bill Clinton told me that he planned to propose model contracts between grain elevator operators and farmers that clearly state the rights and obligations of farmers storing grain in the elevators. These contracts could be distributed through Farm Bureau or the American Agriculture Movement. Clinton also proposed to have both scheduled and surprise state inspections of grain elevators to ensure that grain stored in the elevator that was owned by the farmer had not been sold by the owner of the elevator. And finally, the farmer who has a warehouse receipt or scale ticket should have preferred creditor status, not the banks.

Bill Clinton agreed that lawyers and bankers often wore down the farmers in a bankruptcy case by dragging the case on for years, causing the farmer to drop out leaving more money for the lawyers and bankers when the case is finally resolved. Former Governor Clinton listened more than he talked and thanked me for teaching him and the public about the plight of a farmer that has grain stored in an elevator that goes bankrupt.

The current Governor of Arkansas, at that time, was Frank White. He wrote a letter to President Reagan asking him to release me. He told the President that the information the judge was asking for was already available to him from federal officials that were at the site the day the grain was removed. Governor White said, "The imprisonment of Cryts seems to be an attempt to punish Cryts, rather than a method to find out who helped Cryts."

Bill Emerson had just been elected to Congress as a U.S. Representative from Missouri. He came down to the Pope County Detention Center to meet with me and let me know that he supported me as well. He later introduced H.R. 3984, a bill to give farmers priority when an elevator went bankrupt. Representative Emerson took a personal interest in this situation, because he represented the people in Southeast Missouri who had elected him to office.

In his speech in support of H.R. 3984, Representative Emerson told the members of the House of Representatives:

> One man is responsible for the modest progress that has been made in correcting this flaw. At great personal risk, Wayne Cryts took the extra step that was needed to bring this problem to national attention, and to make it

possible for people like Senator Dole and myself to gain widespread support for remedial legislation.

For taking that step, Wayne Cryts right now sits in a jail in Arkansas. As the result of violating the highly questionable mandates of the Bankruptcy Court, Mr. Cryts has been found guilty of contempt of court-not by a jury, not after a just appeals process, but by the will of a lone bankruptcy judge.

Today, Mr. Cryts is still incarcerated, a prisoner not only of the courts, but his own commitment to real justice. That he violated the letter of the law is not questioned; however, if the intent of the law is fairness and protection of the innocent, he is not guilty.

This excerpt contains the discussion led by Representative Emerson when the Speaker Pro Tempore granted him sixty minutes to speak to the full House of Representatives about the need to reform the bankruptcy code. The full version can be found in the May 13, 1982, Congressional Record, Vol. 128, No. 57.

After I was in jail for about twenty days, the sheriff said, "Wayne, we understand that Bob Dole is requesting that you get a temporary release from jail, so you can testify in Washington, D.C., but, Judge Baker is refusing to let you out."

When Senator Dole's subcommittee found out that the judge refused to let me go, I was notified that the Senate was subpoenaing me. They had ordered me to be in Washington, D.C., on a certain day at a certain time to testify before Senator Dole's subcommittee about the bankruptcy laws involving farmers that had grain stored in grain elevators. Judge Baker still refused to release me from jail. Then, the Judge was contacted by the Justice Department and told that if he did not release me, the Senate was going to find him in contempt of Congress and possibly put him in jail with me. Judge Baker announced to the press that he had decided to allow me a temporary release of three days to go to Washington, D.C., and testify.

As I was lying there in my jail cell that night, I began to think about what I was going to tell those people up there. The next day, I was notified by the U.S. Marshals Office that I was to be freed on my own recognizance for three days and had to return by noon Wednesday. One of my attorneys, Fred Brown, decided to go with me, along with Marvin Meek and Charles Cooper. Fred took Sandy and me down to Little Rock where we boarded a plane and flew to Washington, D.C.

When we got to the Senate building that Monday morning where the hearings were taking place, I couldn't believe the amount of news media that were there to see me. I had never seen so many people with cameras in one place, waiting to take pictures of a plain ol' farmer from the Bootheel of Missouri.

The bankruptcy law was a very emotional issue for some members of the U.S. House of Representatives. The House Judiciary Committee Chairman, Peter Rodino from New Jersey, was very reluctant to revise the Federal Bankruptcy Law because he had worked hard to revise the law in 1978. He did not believe there was anything wrong with the revisions. I told him that the part dealing with grain elevators still had major problems. Representative Rodino refused to allow any revisions to go before the House for consideration that were presented to his committee. Representative Bill Emerson told the members of the House that certain members of the House Judiciary Committee thought the 1978 Bankruptcy Code was written in stone.

When I was notified that it was my turn to testify, I sat down at a table in front of Senator Dole's subcommittee. After the introductions, I said, "Mr. Chairman and members of the committee, I believe that there is more justice in this country than there is anywhere else in the world. But, justice is not always brought and sat in your lap. Sometimes, you have to stand up and reach for it. I believe that for every person that is treated unjustly that will not stand up, the next person that does has to stand a little taller, and reach a little higher. If people who are treated unjustly will not stand up for what is right, then justice will be out of the reach of us all. Mr. Chairman, members of the committee, I sincerely believe that the American farmer is being unjustly treated in these elevator bankruptcys. The law needs to be changed and it needs to be simple enough for two attorneys to take it in separate rooms, read it, and interpret it the same way."

After I made that statement, everyone on the subcommittee busted out laughing. They thought that was the funniest thing they ever heard—that any two lawyers would agree on anything. However, I was serious.

I continued, "We need a law regarding elevators that go bankrupt stating that in a very short period of time, no more than 120 days, a determination of ownership will be made and the private property will be given back to the rightful owners. It should say that a scale ticket or warehouse receipt should be legal claim to that grain. If any of the grain is missing or stolen, then we need something like the FDIC that protects people's money in banks that would pay the farmers out of a fund that had been set up as protection for the farmer."

I believe my comments spurred the process of hearings by the people in Congress to change the bankruptcy law. After I got done with the Senate, I was told that the Chairman of the House Agriculture Committee also requested that I come over and testify before their committee. Since I was supposed to return to jail that Wednesday, they had to contact Judge Baker to tell him they needed an extension through Friday. Judge Baker agreed to the extension and set the time to return at no later than 11:30 a.m. I went over and testified before the House Agriculture Committee. They asked me numerous questions as well and I answered them to the best of my ability. We stayed in Washington, D.C., again that night and flew back to Little Rock Friday. The federal marshals were there to meet me at the airport and take me back to jail.

Senator Bob Dole's committee was able to get the full Senate to vote in favor of remedial amendments to the Federal Bankruptcy Code on three separate occasions, but was unable to get any of them to the floor of the House of Representatives for a vote due to Representative Rodino's refusal to allow it to go before the House for a vote.

Senator Charles Grassley, from Iowa told me that he and Representative Emerson had written President Reagan, asking him to pardon me and to get behind legislation to amend the federal bankruptcy law. I told him that I did not want a pardon from the President, because it would mean that I was guilty of something and I did not believe that I had done anything wrong. I had a warehouse receipt for every bushel of grain that I had deposited and then removed from the elevator.

Later that month, I was informed that President Ronald Reagan had endorsed a Senate passed bill to resolve the grain elevator problems with the federal bankruptcy laws. Whitehouse spokesman, Larry Speakes, told reporters that the president thought it would help prevent dilemmas like the one faced by Mr. Cryts.

The people of the community and farmers from the area were there outside of the jail all the time. Every Sunday morning, they would hold church services at the jail so I could worship with them. The sheriff gave me permission to step outside of the jail in order to do so. I remember a man by the name of Wayne Peterson from South Dakota that led a prayer, asking the Lord to look after me and my family through this terrible ordeal.

A regional news camera crew was there filming church services one Sunday morning. When Judge Baker found out that I was allowed to stand outside the jail to attend church services, he issued a court order forbidding me from attending church. That order didn't go over very well with the people in Russellville. They felt like the judge had overstepped his authority to forbid me from attending church service when I was in no danger of escape and had guards right there by me. This was another indication that the judge was making this thing personal.

While I was in jail, a group of farmers and people that I knew came up to me and one of them said, "Wayne, we want to get rid of the judge."

I said, "We are not going to get rid of him." I was afraid that they were going to hurt him.

Then, he said, "I don't mean get rid of him permanently. It is obvious that the judge is harassing you and we want to harass him a little bit."

I said, "What do you have in mind?"

Ken Crego, who worked for a radio station in Poplar Bluff, Missouri, was the leader of this group. This guy had an incredible gift of gab. I'm telling you if something was black, he could convince you that it was white. He said, "We will keep it in bounds, Wayne. We are not going to physically hurt him or anything."

I said, "Don't do anything that is going to hurt him or scare him to death. And don't put his family in jeopardy either. You know the way I am, I don't want you to do anything that will hurt anybody."

They said, "O.K. We are just going to have some fun with him."

Later that evening, they went to Judge Baker's house in Little Rock to look things over from the street. They got a motel room nearby that evening.

At 2:00 a.m. in the morning, Ken called a plumber and he said, "This is Charles Baker. I live at (he told the plumber the judge's address) and my water line is busted. It is flooding the whole house! We have got to have help immediately! How fast can you get here?"

Ken's girlfriend was in the background hollering, "Charlie! Charlie! The water's coming in on the dining room floor right now!"

Well, that convinced the plumber that this guy was having an emergency. So, the plumber agreed to come to the house.

The last thing Ken said was, "We are going to be in the back of the house. When you get here, just pull up in the driveway, honk the horn and I will come out to get you."

As soon as he hung up, they got in their vehicle and went over to his house so they could watch this all happen. Sure enough, the plumber pulled up in the driveway and "laid" on the horn. They saw the light come on upstairs, and, shortly after that, Judge Baker came to the door. The plumber got out of his vehicle and hurried to the door, but the judge did not let him in. It took the judge a while to convince this guy that he really didn't have a plumbing problem.

Those guys were laughing so hard when they were telling me what happened that I began laughing too. They said that was one of the funniest things they had ever done.

The next thing this group did was call a taxi cab to come to the judge's house at 5:00 a.m. in the morning. Ken called a cab company and said, "This is Charles Baker. I live at (they told the cab company the address) and I've overslept. I am late for the airport. I need you to pick me up immediately! When you pull into the driveway, just honk the horn and I'll come right out."

Then, those guys hurried over to his house to watch what happened. The cab driver came flying into the driveway, honked the horn, and Charles Baker came to the door to see what was going on. The driver got out and walked up to the door to help with the luggage. The judge explained to him that he really didn't need to go to the airport and the cab driver finally left.

The next thing they did was order flowers for his wife and put on the card: Honey, I'm sorry for my transgression and I deeply apologize. If you will forgive me, I'll never do it again.

Next, they ordered pizza for all of the judge's staff for lunch one day. Then, they got as many people as they could to call and order things on a 10-day free trail basis and give them his name and address. He was receiving everything under the sun.

When the media found out about the pranks, they asked the judge about it. The judge told reporters in an interview that he had been the target of pranksters. He reported that anonymous callers had sent plumbers, exterminators, and cab drivers to his house. He also told them that a tow truck had even towed his car away one evening. The reporter stated that Judge Baker laughed at the pranksters and said, "They're just some boys having a good time. I would too, if I were them." But, I think Judge Baker was getting tired of that stuff. Shortly after that he decided to take his family to Europe to get away from everything for a while.

Now, there I was in jail charged with contempt of court, and the only one that could let me out was the judge that had put me in there, and those guys just ran the judge off to Europe!

When they found out the judge was gone, Ken came up to me and said, "Wayne, we have an idea. While the judge is gone, we are going to call a tree service and tell them we are going to build an addition on to our house and we need to remove some shade trees."

I said, "Ken, I don't know. That may be going a little bit too far, I don't think you should do that."

Still, they were really excited about doing that. I don't know if they ever did it or not. I really don't think they did because I read a news article one morning that reported the judge left his mother to "house sit." I was getting to the point that I was actually feeling sorry for the judge. I finally told them that I think he has probably been harassed enough.

When the judge and his family returned from Europe, he ordered me back to court and said, "I've decided to close this case. Therefore, there is no longer any need to keep Mr. Cryts in jail."

Then, he said, "Wayne Cryts is a thief. Such a 'me first' attitude is not consistent with a civilized society. It is obvious to this court that Mr. Cryts envisions himself to be some sort of folk hero who has been called on from on high to right the wrongs inflicted upon farmers when grain elevators fail. His refusal to cooperate should be deemed criminal and Mr. Cryts should be punished for his refusal. In closing this case, I'm going to impose a 'coercive award' of $287,000 against Mr. Cryts, Sandy Cryts, William H. Cryts, Jr., Bill Jewell of Long Lane, Missouri, and Evans Ipock of Buffalo, Missouri, to accumulate at $1,500.00 a day, until it is paid."

Judge Baker did not have the power to charge me with criminal contempt because he was a bankruptcy judge. So, the judge recommended to the U.S. District Court and the U.S. Attorney's office that all five of us be prosecuted for criminal contempt of court.

I was finally released from jail on June 1, 1982, after being in jail over a month. Deputy Sheriff Juanita Henderson of the Pope County Detention Center gave me a scrapbook with pictures and newspaper articles, signed by everyone that worked there. Frank Reynolds, chief deputy sheriff, took me out to lunch at the Marina Inn. He told a reporter, after we ate our lunch, that he wanted to buy me the biggest steak they had. If it had been a 42-ounce steak, he would have bought that. Sheriff Bolin told me that I was one of the nicest prisoners that he had ever met. They all invited me back as a visitor sometime. I had J.D. Gott and Charlie Cooper help me prepare some bottles of Ristine Soybeans labeled "Wayne Cryts Strain" that I signed and gave them as souvenirs.

When I got back home the next day, I was met by my friends, relatives, and reporters. They had tractors with yellow ribbons on them celebrating our return home. They even had a cake that read "Welcome Home Wayne" with an AAM emblem on it.

I was asked to say a few words to the people who were there to welcome us back home. I told them, "It was worth it to go to jail for this cause. The fight is not over yet. There is a long way to go until we reach the finish line."

Then, my wife and I went on vacation for a few days to relax and get some quite time with each other.

The next weekend, Senator Charles Grassley from Iowa was coming to my home to volunteer his time and help me on the farm. The Senator flew into Cape Girardeau Saturday morning and stayed with us on the farm for two days. He wanted to help draw attention to the plight of the American farmer. Senator Grassley was a co-sponsor of a bill passed by the Senate that would give priority to the farmers in grain elevator bankruptcy proceedings. He had even offered to take my place in the Pope County jail, but the judge refused to let him do so.

By the time I was released from jail, the lack of money was becoming a problem again. Interest rates were still high, the cost of production was going up, but the prices of crops were going down. It was becoming harder and harder to make a living on a family farm.

There were a lot of people that wanted to donate money to help me with my legal defense fund. I had already spent about $40,000 of my own money by this time. So Lawrence Tillman, president of Stoddard County Farm Bureau, offered to serve as the collection points for funds as well as an information source to farmers on the pending federal legislation that will help prevent problems like this in the future for farmers. Later, seven county Farm Bureaus in southeast Missouri began accepting funds to aid in my legal defense.

Marvin Meek of Plainview, Texas, President of the American Agriculture Movement, told me that the organization had raised over $25,000 for my defense fund. He said the AAM had a goal of $100,000. Marvin had also been the person that contacted F. Lee Bailey to find out if he would be interested in helping defend me. Mr. Bailey said he wanted $25,000 as retainer up front before he would agree to do so.

Some radio stations had also helped collect donations for my legal defense fund. Two radio stations, KRES-FM and KWIX-AM of Moberly, Missouri, raised $14,836 from farmers, businessmen, and area residents from fifteen counties in the surrounding area. Mike Horne of Russellville who owned KARV in Russellville made the presentation of the funds to me and read a letter from Jerrell Shepherd who operated the station in Moberly. Mr. Shepherd is a Russellville native. Another station, KBOA at Kennett, Missouri, raised $12,000 and a station at Bethany raised $1,500. KULY in Ulysses, Kansas, raised $6,029.

Of course, people in my hometown of Puxico also worked to raise money for my legal defense fund. Mike Hodge and Gail Cookson headed a fundraiser in Puxico that raised $3,316.44. They had an auction and games for the kids. Also, local organizations worked hard to raise money to help us with the legal defense fund.

A defense fund was also set up at the Puxico State Bank. All the money that came in went to this bank and Eddie Sifford, Harley Sentel, and Janet Harmon managed the fund. These three people would review the bills that came in and make the decision as to what bills were to be paid. I never got any of that money for my personal use, nor did I expect to. If I had not had people raising money to help me with my defense to help pay for my lawyers, I would not have been able to afford to hire the lawyers that I needed to represent me in court.

On June 24, 1982, Judge Baker ordered my bank accounts in Risco to be garnished along with nineteen other banks that they thought might have money, property, or other goods that could be used to pay toward the $287,708 judgment issued against me. He also banned any grain elevators from buying or storing any of my grain that would be harvested that fall.

The next thing that Judge Baker tried to do was confiscate my farm equipment. When the word got out about that, the neighbors came in, took my equipment, and scattered with it. I had just gotten back home from an AAM meeting and I discovered that my farm machinery had disappeared. When I asked Sandy about it, she told me that our friends had taken the equipment to their farms to prevent Judge Baker from taking them. When the officers showed up to find out what kind of equipment we had, they couldn't find anything.

I was always amazed that I never had to call any of my neighbors and ask for a favor. They did anything they could to support and protect us. If they thought there was something my family needed, they just took care of it. I've never seen that type of commitment from people for any extended period of time. A lot of these people spent a great deal of money out of their own pockets to help us.

To make matters worse, the Commodity Credit Corporation declared me in default of my loan even though I had tried to pay them by check, cash, and with the commodity itself. They had refused to accept payment each time that I tried to pay them. The president of the bank that my family had used for years, Van Gibbs of Risco, called me the following Monday informing me that the board of directors had authorized him to contact area radio stations and other Missouri media to say that the Cryts farming family had written literally thousands of checks on the bank and each one had been honored. And if the Commodity Credit Corporation would have accepted a check written by Cryts for the repayment of his loan, the check would have been honored.

We were trying to continue to farm during this period of time and it was becoming more and more difficult to do so. By this time, the price of beans was low and the cost of fuel and fertilizer was increasing. I was also getting calls to speak all over the country. I didn't charge them anything for the speaking engagement, because I was not doing this for the money. Sometimes I would get my expenses paid, but that was all I got. The phone seemed to never quit ringing. It was not unusual for it to be 2:00 a.m. in the morning and the phone would ring. It would be a reporter somewhere wanting to do a story. One day, I got a call from a man named Bob Pigott, President of the Chamber of Commerce at Gravette, Arkansas, wanting me to speak to them.

Wayne Gets Set Up at Gravette

When Bob Pigott called me on the phone, he asked me if I would come down to Gravette to speak at the 89th Annual Gravette Day Celebration and be the Grand Marshal of the parade. I told him that I would be happy to. The celebration was to be held on August 15, 1982.

At that time, every vehicle we had was worn out, so Bud Shell loaned me a dark blue van to use on my trip to Gravette. Bud owns a Ford dealership in Dexter, Missouri. He was very helpful to me during this time, loaning me vehicles that I could drive to guest speaking events.

Charlie Cooper went with me on the trip. The festivities were to be that Saturday, so we loaded up the van and drove down the day before. Bob Pigott owned a country and western store there in Gravette and he wanted us to meet him there that evening. When we got there, we went in his store to talk to him. The mayor and several newspaper people were there also. About thirty minutes after we were there, the phone rang. Bob answered the phone, and then told me that the call was for me.

I took the phone and the person on the other end said, "This is George Welch." George was one of the federal marshals who had been sent to the Ristine Elevator and we had gotten well acquainted there. He told me that he had been transferred to the Fort Smith District and that he was the second ranking Marshal-in-Charge.

George said, "Wayne, the judge and the trustee are going to set you up tomorrow to embarrass and discredit you. They asked me to do it, and I told them that I wasn't about to do that and then I told them where to go."

He told me that since he wouldn't do what they wanted, they found a federal marshal that was from Brooklyn, New York, that agreed to do it. His name was Chuck Papachio. Then, George advised me to get my tail back to Missouri.

I said, "I sure appreciate it. Thank you."

When I hung up the phone and turned around, Bob asked who it was that called. Because the room was crowded with lots of people and I did not want them to know that a federal marshal was tipping me off, I told him it was an anonymous phone call and the person told me that Judge Baker and Trustee Robert Lindsey were going to set me up to embarrass and discredit me tomorrow.

I then said, "I don't want anything to happen that would interfere with the Gravette Day Festivities. Charlie and I will head back home if you want us to."

Bob said, "No Wayne, we have advertised this. There are people coming in from all over to hear you speak. If you leave now, it is going to make us look bad. I'm sure it's just some prank caller. There's nothing to it."

Of course, I knew there was something to it, because I knew that George was telling me the truth. But, I figured if the judge and trustee were going to do it, it would happen sooner or later. So, I might as well get it over with.

I said, "If you're sure?"

Bob said, "I'm sure. Let's go on with it like we planned."

Charlie and I stayed with Bob and his wife that night. The next morning, they got up early to go down town to get things started. They were having a marathon race and other activities. Charlie and I got to town around 9:00 a.m.

We hadn't been there fifteen minutes until a federal marshal walked up to me and said, "I'm Federal Marshal Chuck Papachio. Are you Mr. Cryts?"

I said, "Yes sir, I am."

He asked, "Do you have any money or valuables on you?"

"I have my watch, wedding ring, and about $150 in my billfold."

"I am ordering you to turn over all your money and valuables to me."

"No sir. I'm not going to do that."

"Are you refusing a direct order from a federal marshal?"

I said, "Yes sir, I guess I am."

He raised his voice, but didn't get smart. He said, "Mr. Cryts, you do realize that I am a federal marshal?"

"Yes sir."

"For the second time, are refusing a direct order from a federal marshal?"

"Yes sir. I am."

He turned around and walked out the door. Everybody was standing there looking at each other. I was wondering if that was it. Was that all that was going to happen? Bob Pigott was very aggravated about what had happened.

Shortly after that, a guy came running in and said, "Wayne! Wayne! They are getting ready to tow off your van!"

We hurried outside to see what was going on. Marshal Papachio and another federal marshal were standing there with a local deputy sheriff from Benton County named Donald Townsend. They had a wrecker that was driven by Bill McNelly backing up to the van. So, I stepped off the sidewalk and got between the wrecker and the van. The driver continued to back up toward me and I just stood there. The driver of the wrecker finally stopped when he realized I was not going to move.

Marshal Papachio said, "Mr. Cryts, if you don't move, I'm going to arrest you and take you to jail."

Charlie Cooper was standing there audio taping what we were saying.

I said, "Mr. Papachio, I don't want to go to jail, but I can accept going to jail better than what you people are doing to me right now."

There were some people beginning to gather around us and they were not being very pleasant. The word had gotten out that I was being set up. Most of the crowd was aware of this and were getting very upset about what was going on.

Finally, I said, "Marshal Papachio, why don't you let me go ahead and be the Grand Marshal of the parade. After the parade, most of the people will go down to the park and I will come back here. Then, you can arrest me or do whatever you have to do."

He looked around and said, "Listen, I need to call somebody to figure out what I need to be doing." The marshal could see that things were beginning to get out of hand. Then, he said, "All right. You have my word that I won't tow the van until after the parade. I need to call some people."

Charlie said, "I've got that on tape!" But, that didn't seem to bother the federal marshal.

We walked down the street, so I could get on the lead float. As we were walking, I took off my watch, my wedding ring, and took out my billfold and gave everything to Charlie. Then, I got on the float and we started up Main Street. The viewing stand was set up near the place that I had parked the van. When we got to the viewing stand, they stopped to let me off the float so I could watch the rest of the parade from there.

After the parade was over, I could see the wrecker being backed up to the van again. So, I went down there and got between the wrecker and van once again. Marshal Papachio came over and told me that if I didn't get out of the way, he was going to arrest me.

I said, "If you are going to arrest me, you had better do it very quickly and very quietly and you better get us out of town or you are going to have serious trouble on your hands."

So, he handcuffed me, bent my head over, and put me in the back seat of the patrol car. Marshal Papachio got in the back seat with me. The other federal marshal got in the front seat with the local deputy sheriff who was the driver.

By the time we all got in the car, numerous people had surrounded it. They wouldn't let us leave. Someone broke off the antenna and the crowd started rocking the car. I kept telling the marshal that they had better get us out of there. All of a sudden, wham!

The deputy sheriff said, "That was Dan! Dan kicked the patrol car!" He couldn't believe this guy, Dan, kicked the car.

The crowd was getting louder and more upset by the minute.

I said, "You had better get us through this crowd!"

The driver started bumping his way forward through the crowd until he finally got an opening. The marshal had put the handcuffs on me so tight that my fingers were feeling like balloons. I asked him to loosen the handcuffs before my fingers exploded.

He said, "Do I have your word that you are not going to do anything?"

I said, "Hey, I'm not going to do anything."

"I'll uncuff you from behind and cuff you in the front."

When he tried to put the key in the cuffs, he discovered that he had put them on upside down and the key wouldn't go in. So, I had to put my head down in the floorboard of the car in a very awkward position, so he could get it unlocked. Then, he had me move my hands in front of me and cuffed me again.

I asked where we were going and the marshal said, "I'm not going to tell you."

We went down the road a ways and I asked where we were going again. He finally told me that we were going to Fort Smith. Marshal Chuck Papachio told me that he was taking me to the Sebastian County Jail. The marshal said that it was a very tough jail and they have some rough prisoners there. He also told me that if all the prisoners had been good that day, a commissary tray with candy bars, soda, and cigarettes would be pushed around the jail that evening. Then, the prisoners that had money could buy what they wanted.

I said, "Chuck, it's just my luck. I don't have a penny to my name." The marshal looked at me and grinned. He knew that I had given my valuables to Charlie. He said, "I'll loan you ten dollars."

"I appreciate that."

He gave me a ten dollar bill, then looked at his watch and said, "By the time we get there, they will have already served dinner. How long has it been since you had something to eat?"

"I haven't eaten since yesterday evening."

Then, he said, "I don't think we need these handcuffs right now. But, I will have to put them back on before I take you to jail."

Chuck took the handcuffs off and told the deputy to find a place to eat. He said, "We probably don't want to go in, so let's hit a fast food joint."

We found a McDonald's and went through the drive-thru window. We got a Big Mac, French fries, and a soda. I felt like I was about to starve to death! When we finished eating, I told Chuck that I really appreciated it.

When we got to the jail, he put the handcuffs back on and we went inside. They processed me in, fingerprinted me, and took my mug shot. Then, they gave me a dirty, filthy uniform to put on. It had blue and white stripes that circled the uniform. In other words, it was ugly and nasty. Then, they gave me a tin cup. The jailer told me that I really needed to hang on to that tin cup. I found out later that the jailer's name was Bill.

When I finished changing into my prison uniform, they took me upstairs to the jail cells. There was a long row of cells, and we walked down them a little ways before they stopped and opened one of the cell doors. The guard told me to go on in and then he slammed the door shut behind me. When I was growing up on the farm, I never dreamed that I would hear that sound from the inside of a cell. I turned around and looked back outside the bars. It was a scary feeling. Then, I looked around in the cell and saw that there were eight bunks in that cell. And seven of the bunks were filled already. As I looked at each one of the men in there, I realized that they were all Cubans. They couldn't speak a word of English and I couldn't speak Spanish. So, I knew we were not going to be able to talk to each other. There was one bunk vacant and it was an upper bunk.

Some of those guys were pretty rough looking and I began to get worried about that. I had seen TV shows about people being in situations like this that didn't have a good ending.

I thought to myself, "If I'm going to survive, I had better make these folks think I'm the meanest person that ever walked."

So, I looked around for the biggest one in there. He was lying on a bottom bunk under the bunk that was empty. I strutted around there for a little bit making some noise and trying to act as mean as I possibly could. Then, I walked straight over to the big guy; pointed at him, tapped him on the shoulder and said, "Out!" He didn't move, so I reached down, grabbed him by the arm, and pulled him up out of the bunk. He just stood there looking at me, along with the others. I pointed to the top bunk, made him get up in it, and I took his.

Sometime around 11:00 that night, my cellmates decided that I probably wasn't near as tough as I was acting and they were beginning to start in on me.

Then, all of a sudden a jailer came to the door, unlocked it, and said, "Cryts, come out here!"

I shot out of there like a bullet and was happy to do so. He slammed the door behind me and locked it back. Then, told me to follow him. We walked around to the other side to another row of cells that had solid doors on the front of them. They all had a flapper in the middle of the door that was used to pass food in to the prisoners. I thought those cells must be for the ones that were really violent and hoped that I was going to get one by myself.

We walked down to the third door. The jailer stopped, unlocked the door, and opened it. I could barely make out a little light bulb hanging down from the ceiling, but it was not on. The only thing that I could see was that there were two bunks on each side with someone on each of the bottom bunks. There was a black guy lying on the left bottom bunk and another black guy lying on the right bottom bunk. The two upper bunks were empty, which meant I was going to have to climb up on one of those. Just then, the jailer put his hands on my back, shoved me in the cell, and slammed the door. When that door shut, I couldn't see a thing. It was so dark in there that I could not see my hand in front of my face. I felt like I had gone from the frying pan to the fire.

I thought to myself, "They have put me in this cell, so these guys can kill me!" I really thought, "This was it!"

I backed up against the door and stood there, just waiting for something to happen. I was terrified and didn't know what to do.

I thought to myself, "If they move, I'm going to kick, bite, and anything else that I can in order to survive." I knew that I had no choice.

I could hear them moving a little bit. Then, they mumbled something to each other. But, I could sense that they were not getting up. They were just lying there. I don't know how long I stood there, but I felt like a coil spring ready to explode if I felt either one of them make a move toward me.

Finally, after standing there against that door for a few hours, I was plumb give out and thought to myself, "If they were going to do something, they would have done it by now."

I took my hand, put it on the upper bunk, slid it along the edge, and walked as quietly as I could until I got to the corner of the bunk. I reached down to feel for the corner of the lower bunk and put my foot on it. Then, I stood there for a little bit to see if anything was going to happen. When I didn't hear anything, I pulled myself up and rolled over on the bunk. I lay very still, so I could hear any movement or sound. I kept running my hand down the frame of the bunk, because I knew that they would have to put their hand on it if they were going to do anything. But, I never felt or heard anything the rest of the night. I finally fell asleep some time later in the night through pure exhaustion.

I woke up early that morning when I heard my cellmates moving around. The guy that was sleeping under my bunk was the first to get up. He looked at me and said, "Who are you?"

I said, "I'm Wayne Cryts."

He told me that his name was Jim. I don't remember what his last name was. Then, he introduced the other prisoner to me. We talked for a while and Jim asked, "What are you in for?"

I said, "I got into a little scrape with some federal marshals."

"Federal marshals! What did you do?"

"It's a long story, Jim. If I get time, I'll tell you all about it."

Then, we heard someone coming down the hall. It was the jailer. He stopped at our door, opened it, and said, "Wayne, come out here. We have decided to make you a trustee."

I said, "Thank you, I appreciate that."

He said, "Jim knows the routine, just follow him around, and do whatever he tells you to do."

I told him that I could do that. Jim told me that our job was to push the drink tray around to all the prisoners. We went to each cell and when we stopped, they would hold their tin cup out of the cell. They could have milk, orange juice, or lukewarm coffee. I found out then how important that tin cup was to the prisoners. Jim and some other guy were on kitchen detail, so I helped clean the kitchen. When we finished cleaning the kitchen, we went back to our cell.

We sat there for a while talking, and then Jim lifted up his mattress. He showed me a butcher knife that he had stolen out of the kitchen. I didn't want to see that! Jim didn't say a word about it and I didn't either. He just showed me the knife and covered it up again. I'm not sure why he felt like he had to show it to me. He may have just been proud of it or he may have been trying to intimidate me. As I got to know my cellmates, I discovered that they were pretty nice guys and I was mighty grateful for that; especially when I found out Jim had that butcher knife.

Later that afternoon, the Sebastian County Sheriff requested to see me in his office. We talked for most of the afternoon about what I had gone through at Gravette the day before and the removal of my grain at Ristine. He told me that they had received numerous calls from some very upset people in Gravette for what had happened. Then, he told me that he would be glad when I got out of there.

I said, "You and me both!"

When we finished talking, he had me escorted back to my cell.

That evening after dinner, the guard came by and told me to take the commissary tray around to the prisoners. I did what I was told and pushed the tray around to the prisoners. They could have a drink, candy bar, and cigarettes if they had the money. When I was finished pushing the tray around, I bought a candy bar and a pack of cigarettes for myself from the commissary tray. I hadn't smoked in a while and I figured that I was entitled to it. I finally made it through my first full day in jail there, which was a Sunday.

I couldn't sleep that night because of all the cockroaches that were crawling around on me and in the cell. I stayed up all night killing them and was told that I had set a record for killing the most cockroaches in one night with a total of 280. When the *Arkansas Traveler Magazine* heard about it, they published a cartoon of me sitting on my cell bunk with my AAM cap on with cockroaches crawling around on it. Then, they had a big pile of cockroaches on the floor and a mark on the wall for everyone that I had killed. A reporter asked me what the secret of my success was and I told him that I thought it was my pointed toed cowboy boots, because the cockroaches could not get in the corners and get away from me. They had a big laugh about that.

The next morning, the Head Marshal, Mack Burton, from that area came over and got me. He had another marshal with him, but I can't remember his name. They took me over to the Federal Court House and upstairs to their section of the building. They had started processing me in and getting my fingerprints, when George Welsh walked in. As he walked over to me, I cannot describe to you the look that he had on his face. You would have to have seen it for yourself. He was ashamed of the way I was being treated and for what they were doing to me. He knew that I had been set up, but was helpless to do anything about it.

"Wayne, my office is right there and I want to talk to you when they get done processing you," George said, pointing at the door.

I said, "O.K."

When they were finished with me, whoever was processing me in at that time heard what George said and let me go to his office. So, I went in and sat down. Just as George started to talk to me, the head marshal walked in. He walked straight over to me, grabbed me by the arm, and literally jerked me out of the chair! Then, he half dragged me back through the processing room and over to a holding cell. He opened the door, shoved me in the cell, and slammed the door. Then, he turned around and went back down the hallway.

I leaned over and looked down the hallway to see what Marshal Burton was going to do next. I could see that he went straight to George's office, stepped in, said something, and then went over to his office. Whatever he said must have made George mad, because he came out of his office and quickly went across the hallway to the head marshal's office. I could hear George and the head marshal talking very loudly to each other. George was cussing the head marshal and told him that he was a sorry SOB for what they were doing to me.

Then, I heard the head marshal say, "George, you better watch that mouth of yours! I'm telling you that you had better watch it!"

Finally, I saw George walk back to his office. A few minutes later, George walked back over to Marshal Burton's office and cussed him out again!

A short while after all that had happened, George walked back to my cell with a cup of coffee. His hands were visibly shaking as he handed the coffee to me through the bars of the cell.

George said, "If I didn't have so many years invested, I would resign today for what they are doing to you."

I said, "George, you have helped me so much in so many ways, I don't hold any of this against you at all."

"I appreciate that Wayne. I just want you to know that I am sorry for what they are doing to you."

"I know that you have done everything that you can to help me and I appreciate it."

At about 8:30 that morning, Marshal Burton came in and took me to the courtroom downstairs. George wouldn't go with them, because he did not want to have any part of what they were going to do. We walked in the courtroom and there was a prosecutor and three federal marshals already there. The head marshal and I sat down at the defense table and the prosecutor was setting at his table. We were all waiting for the judge to come in. While we were waiting, I found out the judge's name was Franklin McWaters and that he was a Federal Magistrate Judge.

A few minutes later, the door opened, and Judge McWaters walked in. Usually, when a judge walks in, everybody stands up until he sits down, but that did not happen this time. He walked over to his table and set down. Then, he looked around and said, "I'm going to need a little bit of help with this case. I don't even have a file number on it."

The prosecutor stood up and said, "Your Honor, we want to know how Mr. Cryts is going to plead?"

Judge McWaters looked at me and said, "Mr. Cryts how do you plead?"

I said, "Not guilty."

The prosecutor said, "Not guilty!"

I said, "Yes, not guilty."

The prosecutor tapped his fingers on the table for a bit, while he sat there thinking. Finally, the judge said to the prosecutor, "Well, what do you recommend?"

The prosecutor looked around and said, "I guess we can release him on his own recognizance."

Judge McWaters said, "Fine. Mr. Cryts, you are going to be released on your own recognizance with a $1,000 unsecured bond." Then, wham! Judge McWaters struck the gavel, got up, and walked out.

I had not been read my rights and had just been arraigned in a federal court before a federal judge without legal representation and had no idea what I had been charged with. Now, I'm not the smartest person in the world, but I knew that was not right.

I had been released on my own recognizance in Fort Smith and I didn't know anyone. I had not been allowed to call my attorney. On top of that, I had no money to call anyone with and I had no vehicle, because they confiscated my van. And I had no idea where the van was either. So, I didn't know what I was going to do. Then, I saw Charlie walking toward me. I don't know how he found me, but I sure was glad to see him. I wasn't surprised, however, because Charlie used to be a newspaper reporter and knew how to find things out.

Charlie asked me what was going on? I explained everything that had just happened to me in the courtroom that morning. He said, "You've been arraigned in court without a lawyer and you don't even know what you have been charged with?"

I said, "Yes, that about sums it up."

Charlie said, "Wayne, you have got to be kidding! They can't do stuff like that."

"Well Charlie, I'm telling you that is just what has happened and I've been released on my own recognizance."

"Wayne, this can not be happening!"

"I know it Charlie, but it is."

Then, Charlie told me that he had called my attorney and Homer Evans back in Puxico to tell them what was going on. Charlie also told me that he had told them to tell Sandy that I had been arrested, so she could call me. He knew that Sandy would be at the Puxico Homecoming and it might be hard to find her. So, Homer had George Foster to find Sandy and tell her what had happened.

I asked Charlie where he had been and he said he was with the mayor of Gravette all weekend. He said the mayor helped him find out where I was and had a friend bring him over there this morning. Charlie told me that the people in Gravette were very unhappy about what had happened over there this weekend and that they had been calling the sheriff's office and anyone in a government position from the governor on down to complain about it. He also told me that the marshal had given Bob Pigott a "writ" garnishing any money the Chamber of Commerce may have intended to give me for participating in the celebration and they were very unhappy about that too.

Charlie asked where the van was and I told him that I had no idea. I asked how we were going to get home. I did not want Sandy driving down to get us, because I was afraid the judge and trustee would do the same thing to her. He said that Carlos Welty was coming down here to get us. Carlos was a very good friend of the family and a vice president in the American Ag Movement in Missouri. When Carlos got there later that day, we got in the vehicle and headed back to Missouri. On the way home, I explained what had happened in court that morning and he could not believe it either.

When we got back home, I called Bud Shell and told him what had happened to the van and that the judge did not intend to give the van back. I told him that the judge said it would be sold to help pay the debt that I owed. He told me not to worry about it, because he would get it back.

Trial in Fayetteville

My family and I were busy harvesting our crops when I received a notice that I had to go to court on Monday, October 11, 1982, on the charge of interfering with a federal marshal. I went to Caruthersville, Missouri, the next day to visit with a lawyer over there by the name of Jim Ed Reeves to see if he would represent me.

He said, "Wayne, I have fought on both sides of the same issue so many times and won, but I don't know how to fight a case like this. You are fighting for justice and that's not what I do. I'm afraid I can't help you."

I said, "O.K., thank you for your time," and went back home.

Sandy and I talked about who we should contact next and I said, "The best lawyer that I know is C.H. Parsons in Dexter."

I called and set up an appointment to meet with him. I told C.H. that I had been charged in Fayetteville, Arkansas, with obstruction of justice and I have requested a jury trial. The judge granted my request and I need a lawyer.

C.H. said, "Wayne, I can't do you any good in Arkansas, because I don't know the judges or the prosecutors down there. However, I do have a good friend down there by the name of Bill Wilson and he is an outstanding lawyer! I don't know if he will take your case or not, but I would be glad to call him for you, if you would like for me to."

I told him that I would appreciate it.

C.H. said, "I'll call you and let you know if he will take your case, and if he does, you can give him a call to set up an appointment."

A few days later, C.H. Parsons called me and said, "Wayne, I've talked to Bill Wilson and he is willing to talk to you. He wants you to give him a call and tell him what happened."

I called Bill Wilson, introduced myself, and told him the whole story about what I had been through. Then, I said, "C.H. Parsons said you were a good friend of his and that you might be interested in taking my case."

Mr. Wilson said, "Yes, I would be interested in talking to you about it. I am familiar with Judge McWaters. I think I can plea bargain this case for you, so you won't have to serve any time, but you will probably have to pay a fine."

I said, "No sir, Mr. Wilson. You don't understand. I don't want to plea bargain, because I'm not guilty of anything."

"Mr. Cryts, you need to realize that you are in an indefensible position on this."

"What do you mean?"

"You have been charged with obstruction of justice, because you refused a direct order from a federal marshal. Now, did you refuse a direct order from a federal marshal?"

I said, "Yes."

Then, Mr. Wilson said, "How can I defend you? You are guilty of what you have been charged with."

"Bill, the judge and trustee set me up!"

"Wayne, I don't want to hear it. That has nothing to do with the case."

That really let the wind out of my sails. Then, I asked, "How can a jury find me guilty when I was set up by the judge and trustee?"

He said, "Wayne that has nothing to do with the case. Did you or did you not refuse a direct order from a federal marshal?"

I said, "Yes, I did."

Then, he said, "You're guilty!"

I said, "Mr. Wilson, I will not plead guilty to this! I have requested a jury trail and have been given one. If a jury finds me guilty, I won't like it, but I will accept it."

He said, "They will find you guilty and I am going to tell you what will happen to you. The jury will have no choice but to find you guilty, because you are guilty. Furthermore, I have nothing to defend you with. You are going to serve a minimum of twenty years hard time. Do you understand what hard time means?"

I said, "I can't understand why I would be sentenced to twenty years of hard time."

Bill said, "You don't even understand what you have done, do you?"

I said, "Well, I guess not. What are you referring to?"

He said, "Have you ever heard the story 'The Emperor Has No Clothes'?"

I told him that I had not.

Bill then said, "A federal judge's power is his court orders. Judge Baker issued you a court order not to remove the grain and you violated that court order. Then, the federal marshals, FBI, and law enforcement officers refused to uphold his court order by stopping you. In doing so, you stripped that judge naked of his power. You sent shockwaves throughout the judicial system. They are going to make an example of you one way or another. They have maneuvered you into breaking a law in a way that you have no defense for. Do you understand that?"

I said, "I hadn't thought about it that way nor did I have any intentions of doing that to the judge."

Then, Bill said, "They had a psychiatrist analyze your personality to predict what you would do when they did that. They knew you would refuse to give up your wedding ring, because it had sentimental value to you. And when you refused that direct order, you were guilty of obstruction of justice."

I said, "Mr. Wilson that may very well be, but I will not plead guilty to this. If you do not want to represent me and I can not find a lawyer that will, I will represent myself."

He was quiet for a long time and finally he said, "Mr. Cryts, I believe everyone deserves his day in court. If you want me to represent you, I will do it. However, I want you to understand that you are in an indefensible position and they will find you guilty. The second thing I want you to understand is I'm not crazy like you damn farmers. I don't work for nothing. I want you to put up $16,000 as a retainer, and then I'll take your case."

I said, "Fine."

Sandy and I went to Fayetteville to meet with Mr. Wilson and discuss the case in more detail. The whole time I was there, he tried to get me to plea bargain. But, I refused. We went to court on October 11, 1982. The first thing we did was select the jury. The judge informed us that he would be questioning the perspective jurors. I thought that was a bit unusual, because the lawyers representing each side usually do the questioning themselves. My lawyer had been given the names of all the people that would be considered for the jury. The prosecutor was allowed to remove six people and we were allowed to remove six. Then, we would have twelve jury members plus one alternate.

My lawyer, Bill Wilson, had an index card on each one of the perspective jurors with a little history about them on it. It told their name, age, whether or not he or she went to church, his or her occupation, and if he or she ever fought the system in any way. There was a lot of information on those cards. He had the cards laid out on the defense table in front of us and when Judge McWaters would question a juror, we would look at their bio card to see if that person was one that we wanted on the jury or one that we definitely did not want. Then, he would note it on the card with a "yes" or "no."

We were going through the lists and saw that one guy had received a speeding ticket and he had fought that thing forever, trying to win. Bill Wilson said, "We want that guy." So, we put a "yes" by his name.

Every once in a while, we would have one that we just couldn't read and we would put a question mark on that person's card. Then, it came down to this one last guy. He was a sharp looking guy, crew cut, and dressed immaculately. This guy is a retired Army Colonel. Bill Wilson said, "What do you think about him?"

I said, "I think he would be good. We definitely want him."

Bill said, "You have got to be out of your mind! He is a retired Army Colonel. Do you remember what you have been charged with?"

I said, "Yes, obstruction of justice and refusing a direct order."

Bill said, "What is drilled into the military people ever day they are there?"

I said, "To obey orders."

Bill said, "Wayne, do you realize that if you had him on the jury, he would probably be the foreman because he would take charge. And you would be guilty before we even started. You would have no chance of being found not guilty!"

I never even thought about that. The guy looked like an honest, clean cut person that I consider myself to be. And I would imagine that he was, but he was not the type of person that I needed on the jury. Anyway, we put a "no" by his name. When the process was over, we selected the six we wanted to be on the jury that had a "yes" by their name and the Colonel was not one of them.

The prosecutor also had his list of cards with those on it that he did not want and you guessed it, the guy that had fought the system was one of them. They knew the prospective jurors backgrounds too. When my lawyer and the prosecutor finished rejecting six jurors each, we looked at the cards we had left and every one of them had a question mark on it. So, I had a jury that we were unsure of, but I still had faith in the system. I felt like a jury of my peers was my only hope. I do believe that we have justice in this country, but the average person can't afford it. If it hadn't been for all the people that raised money to put in my legal defense fund, I would not have had a lawyer like Bill Wilson.

After the jury was selected, the trial started. A special prosecutor by the name of Bear Jackson was brought in to handle the case. It was my understanding that he had the best conviction rate of any federal prosecutor in the United States. So, he was brought in to slam the door on me.

The prosecutor started calling in witnesses. He would begin by asking the witnesses if they saw me there that day and they would say "yes." Then, he would ask if they heard the federal marshal give me a direct order to turn over my personal possessions to him and they would say "yes." Then, he would ask if they heard him identify himself again and ask if I was refusing a direct order from a federal marshal? They would say "yes."

I remember one of the people that the prosecutor had on the witness stand was the deputy sheriff from Gravette and his name was Donald Townsend. The prosecutor asked him a series of questions, which basically everybody knew the answers to because they had heard them before. The prosecutor, then asked the deputy sheriff if he had witnessed any acts of violence?

Deputy Townsend said, "Yes I did."

The prosecutor said, "Would you tell the ladies and gentlemen of the jury what you witnessed?"

The deputy said, "When the federal marshals arrested Mr. Cryts and were putting him in the car, I saw this little old lady repeatedly hit the federal marshal with her pocket book."

The jury got tickled over this and started laughing. Well, that made the judge and prosecutor mad as you can imagine since he was their witness.

One of the things that really disturbed me was the testimony of one of the federal marshals. When this marshal was on the witness stand, the prosecutor asked him, "Where were you when Marshal Papachio approached Mr. Cryts and asked for his personal possessions?"

He said, "I was stationed behind Bob Pigott's store with my gun drawn."

I guess they were expecting me to run out the back door. That answer concerned me when I heard that, because I have always wondered if he intended to shoot me if I had indeed run out the back door.

Then, the prosecutor called me to the witness stand and I was sworn in. The prosecutor asked me a series of questions that I answered yes to. Then he asked, "Did you refuse a direct order from a federal marshal?"

I said, "Yes I did."

Then, I looked over at Bill Wilson and he was sitting at the table with his head in his hands. He knew the prosecutor had me then, but I answered every question as truthfully as I possibly could. When Bear Jackson was finished questioning me, I went back to the defense table and sit down.

Bill leaned over and said, "Wayne, you're the best witness the prosecutor has had so far."

Then, Bill presented the defense and that finished up the testimony of the trial.

After each lawyer was given an opportunity for a final summation, Judge McWaters addressed the jury. He said, "Ladies and gentlemen of the jury, this is a criminal proceeding and I will not accept a 'hung' jury. This must be a unanimous decision. I will not accept any thing other than a unanimous decision."

After a pause, the judge continued, "I want to tell the ladies and gentlemen of the jury one thing. If you come back with anything other than a guilty verdict, we might as well throw our laws out the window, everybody strap on a six gun, and go down the street shooting!"

That was the last thing the jury heard as they filed out of the courtroom. Then, Judge McWaters recessed the court until the jury reached its verdict.

Sandy and I went out in the hall. I just backed up to the wall and slid down it to the floor. Then, Bill came over and said, "Wayne, we'll appeal this."

I said, "No Bill, I don't want it appealed. I have had my opportunity to go before a jury. Again as I told you before, if they come back with a guilty verdict, I won't like it, but I will accept it, whatever the penalty."

He said, "Well, I don't know what we would appeal it on anyway."

Then, he walked over to a bench and sat down.

Sandy and I were talking and I said, "Dad and Mom will help you with the kids."

After what the judge said to the jury before they left, I just knew that I was going to be sent away for at least twenty years. Everything seemed to have gone the prosecutor's way. Bear Jackson had done a good job.

I don't know how long we were there before the jury came back in, but finally the bailiff came out and said, "Wayne, the jury has reached a verdict."

We went back in and sat at the defense table and Bill said, "Wayne, whatever you do, don't show any emotion when the verdict is read."

I said, "All right."

The jury came back in and Judge McWaters said, "Ladies and gentlemen of the jury, have you reached your verdict?"

The jury foreman said, "Yes, Your Honor we have."

The judge said, "Would you pass it to the Bailiff?"

The Bailiff walked over, got the piece of paper that they had written their verdict on, and took it up the judge. He opened it up and said, "Was this a unanimous decision?"

The jury foreman said, "Yes, Your honor, it was."

Judge McWaters said, "Are you positive this is a unanimous decision?"

The jury foreman said once again, "Yes, Your Honor."

Then, the judge asked him one more time, "Are you sure this was a unanimous decision?"

And the jury foreman said again, "Yes, Your Honor, it was."

Instead of handing the paper back to the bailiff as the judge should have, he just threw it down on the floor. The bailiff walked over, picked it up, looked at it, and said, "The ladies and gentlemen of the jury find the defendant not guilty."

There was a roar in the court room when the crowd heard the verdict.

You can't imagine what was going through my mind at that time. My whole future and life was in the hands of that jury. Most people have no comprehension what a person goes through in those hours that are spent waiting for the jury to make a decision. When that bailiff said "not guilty," my lawyer broke down and cried.

The prosecutor, Bear Jackson, jumped up and said, "Your Honor, I demand a poll of this jury."

This meant that each one of the jurors had to stand up and tell his or her name and state his or her verdict. Each one of them stood up, stated their name, and said, "Not guilty!"

Judge McWaters just sat there in disbelief. I thought he was going to overrule the jury himself. Finally, he said, "Court dismissed," and slammed the gavel down on the desk. Then, he got up and headed out of the courtroom.

I was in a state of shock and disbelief myself. I started to get up and go over to Sandy and then I thought, "My van! I wanted my van back. Bill, Bill, Bill tell the judge to release the van back to me!"

He said, "O.K."

Judge McWaters had just started through the door into his chambers and Bill said, "Your Honor, Your Honor!" The Judge turned and looked over his shoulder at Bill. Then, Bill said, "Mr. Cryts requests that you release the van to him."

Judge McWaters said, "It will be a cold day in hell when I release that van," and he walked on into his chambers. You can't imagine the emotions of relief and excitement in that room. Everyone was hugging and kissing each other! I felt like the weight of the world had just been lifted off of me.

They finally released the van six weeks later, but we had a difficult time finding out where it was. They finally told us that it was in Bentonville, Arkansas, and we drove down to pick it up. Some guy had it parked in his shed. We presented the papers to him, got in it, and headed back home. On the way back, I was stopped by an Arkansas State Highway Patrolman for speeding. The patrolman got out of his car, walked up to my door, and asked for my driver's license. So, I gave him my license and he took it back to his car to do the routine background check. I guess they told him who I was, too.

When he came back to the car, he said, "Mr. Cryts, I don't blame you for wanting to get out of Arkansas, but I would advise you to drive a little slower on your way out."

He talked to us for about thirty minutes before he let us go. I thanked him for not writing me a ticket and headed for Puxico.

Criminal Contempt of Court Filed Against Cryts

A short time after the trial at Fayetteville concluded, I was notified that Judge G. Thomas Eisele had requested that U.S. Attorney George Proctor file a charge of criminal contempt of court against me. Earlier, Judge Eisele said that Judge Baker did not have the authority to levy a judgment against me and he had set aside that judgment of $287,000. Since the U.S. attorney did have the authority, this new charge would take the place of Judge Baker's.

I thought I was finished with that whole thing. Now, we had another trial to go through. I called my lawyer, Bill Wilson, and told him about the notice that I had received, stating that I was going back to court.

Bill said, "Wayne, I don't know how we lucked out down there last time and you were found innocent. But, let me tell you, it won't happen two times in a row. Judge Eisele was voted the most outstanding trial judge in the United States in 1976. Let me plea bargain this for you."

I said, "No Bill. I will not plea bargain."

The court date was set and I let Bill know when it was. A few days later, the phone rang and Sandy said it was Bill Wilson.

I picked up the phone and he said, "Wayne, I talked to Judge Eisele and we reached a plea bargain agreement."

I said, "Bill…"

He interrupted me and said, "You will just get a token sentence, a fine, and it will be over with."

I said, "No. I'm not going to do that Bill. I'm not ten percent guilty and ninety percent innocent. I'm either one hundred percent right or I'm one hundred percent wrong. I will not plea bargain. I want a jury to decide if I'm guilty or not. Again, as I told you during the last trial, if the jury says I'm guilty, then I will suffer the penalty. If they say I'm innocent, then I'm innocent."

"Wayne, I want to tell you right now that this is the very best advice that I can give you. If you are not going to take my advice, then I'm resigning as your lawyer."

That just crushed me, because I had a tremendous amount of confidence in Bill and I really like him. When I first met Bill Wilson, he had a full beard and it looked good on him. He had the perfect face for a full beard. But, he shaved that beard off before the trial at Fayetteville. He said, "Those people over there are very conservative and if I wear a beard in that courtroom it might prejudice the jury." That's how far he went as a lawyer to defend me and now he is quitting me.

The trial was coming up in two weeks and my lawyer quit on me. I was just devastated. I told Sandy that I was going to talk to Bob Hardin. He was kind of the person that I leaned on when things got tuff. I talked to him about my troubles for most of the day. I guess it was about 2:00 a.m. in the morning when I got back to the house. Sandy was still up waiting for me and she told me that Bill Wilson had been calling.

She said, "Bill wanted you to call him no matter what time it was when you got in."

I was so upset with him that I started to go on to bed. I was still hurt that he had resigned. But, I finally picked up the phone and called Bill.

He said, "Wayne, I have decided that I want to be your lawyer on this case if you will have me back."

I came very close to telling him no. But, I thought to myself, "Wayne, you need a lawyer, and he is probably as good as you are going to get."

I said, "Bill, I want you to know this. If you want to be my lawyer again that will be fine, but to me, at this point, you are just another damn lawyer and I have absolutely no respect for you anymore."

I could tell that hurt him, because I could just hear it in his voice. He paused a moment and said, "I want back on the case."

I said, "Fine. I appreciate that."

Then, he told me that he would call me back in the morning.

After I thought about what he had told me, I realized that Bill was doing what he thought was best for me. He really didn't think I could win this case and didn't want me to go to jail. I was sorry that I had responded to him in that way. I do have a tremendous amount of respect for him.

When Bill called back the next day he said, "Wayne, it's going to take a lot of preparation for this trial, because it is going to be the toughest thing you have ever gone through. You have been charged with criminal contempt."

I said, "What is criminal contempt?"

Bill said, "It's a little vague. I'm not sure that I really understand what criminal contempt is myself. But, that's what you are charged with." Then, Bill asked me to come down to his office to begin preparing for the case.

In the mean time, Charlie Schollenberger, a reporter for the *Kansas City Times*, met with me. He told me that he covers the court news in Kansas City. We talked about the case for quite a while.

During the conversation, Charlie said, "Wayne, I would give anything if you would let me observe you and your lawyer while you are preparing for this case."

I said, "Charlie, if you give me your word that you won't use anything we say while we are preparing for the trial, I'll let you sit in on it. And anything that is said behind closed doors is off the record. You will have to get your story from whatever happens in the courtroom."

He said, "Wayne, you have my word. I will not divulge anything that goes on between you and your lawyer."

We went down to Bill Wilson's office and I told him that Charlie Schollenberger was out in the waiting room. I explained to Bill that he was a reporter from Kansas City who wanted to sit in on our preparation for the trial and I told him that would be fine with me.

Bill said, "Wayne, you have got to be out of your mind! You can't possibly let a reporter in here. If the prosecutor finds out what our strategy is we're done!"

I said, "Bill, he gave me his word that everything we say in here is off the record."

He said, "Wayne!"

I interrupted him and said, "It's O.K."

Then, he said, "All right. It's your funeral. If you want the reporter in here that's fine."

Charlie sat in on all of our meetings and observed the process we went through to prepare for the trial. After the trial was over, Charlie told me that he had learned more about what goes on in our justice system while sitting with me and my lawyer behind closed doors than he had ever known in all the times that he covered court proceedings from the courtroom, and he thanked me for trusting him.

Bill was prepping me for the upcoming trial that was to begin the following week. He had several boxes of depositions and transcripts from the trials that I had been in before.

He said, "Wayne, I want you to take these boxes home and read everything in there. When the prosecutor gets you on the witness stand, if you deviate from these one little bit, he is going to nail you to the wall. Do you understand how important this is? You have got to answer the questions the same way."

I just pushed them back and said, "Bill, I don't need them."

He said, "Wayne, don't you understand how important this is? If we lose this case, you will go to jail."

I said, "When you tell the truth, you don't have to remember what you said before, because it's always there."

He said, "Fine!"

Then, we got started studying the biographies of the prospective jurors. The jury was selected using the same process we had used in the previous trial. After the jury was selected, the trial began.

They wanted to convict me this time so badly that the government subpoenaed my Dad as a witness against me. They wanted my dad to get on the witness stand and say, "Yes. I saw my son, Wayne Cryts, removing the grain out of the Ristine Elevator." Dad would be under oath and they knew that he had to answer the questions truthfully or risk perjuring himself. They thought that if the jury heard my own dad saying, "Yes, my son did this," then it would really have an impact on the jury. They paid all Dad's expenses, motel, food, and travel to be there and testify against me.

On the day of the trial, the prosecutor called my Dad to the witness stand. He said, "Mr. Cryts, on February 16, 1981, at an elevator north of New Madrid called Ristine, did you see your son remove grain from that elevator?"

Dad set there a little bit and he said, "Well, let me tell you how I have to answer this question. When I was a small child, we had corn cob fights. On one occasion, when I was up in the loft of the barn, a kid hit me with this old, wet, muddy corn cob and I fell out of the loft on my head. I have had a hard time remembering things after that."

Then, he had told them that he had the measles and began to go through every childhood illness that he had had while he was growing up. I could see that the prosecutor was becoming impatient and even wanted to object, but this was his witness and he had asked the question. Dad then began to tell them about a car wreck that he had been in. A drunk driver had hit him head on and everyone thought he was dead, but he pulled through. As a result of the accident, he had to wear a cast for eighteen months on his leg because it did not heal properly. And then, he told everyone that he had had open heart surgery. He pulled up his shirt and said, "They cut me from here to here and just ripped me open." He finally got to the cataract surgery that he had about a year ago and told them about that. He told them that after the surgery, he was able to see much better.

About an hour and a half later, Dad finally said, "Now, I will answer your question. On February 16, 1981, I was at the Ristine Elevator, but I couldn't really see very well and I have a hard time remembering details."

When the prosecutor realized that he was not going to be able to get my Dad to say anything against me he said, "I have no more questions for this witness, Your Honor."

Dad stepped down from the witness stand and they called me to the stand next. I was sworn in and the prosecutor started brow beating me and trying to make a fool out of me.

Then, he said, "Ladies and gentlemen of the jury, I want to advise you not to ever get on a ship with this man. If it starts to sink, he will take every life boat, and leave everybody else to go down with the ship."

He went on and on like this. Finally, he asked me if I had taken the grain out of the Ristine Elevator?

I said, "Yes Sir. I did."

Then, he said, "Mr. Cryts, shortly after you removed the grain from the MFA Elevator at Bernie, you began depositing $999.99 money orders in your account. Would you please tell the ladies and gentlemen of the jury why you did that?"

I said, "To keep the thieving, money hungry lawyers from getting my money."

A hush went through the courtroom and I could see that the prosecutor and judge had gotten upset with that answer.

Then, the prosecutor said, "Mr. Cryts, I want you to quit lying and tell the members of the jury exactly why you did that. You did this so you could run for political office, didn't you?"

I said, "I'm very proud of the battle that I'm fighting and I'm very proud of my reputation. I do not want to ruin my reputation by becoming a politician." The jury just burst out laughing when they heard that.

Then, he turned around and went back to his table, picked up a newspaper, came back over to me, and said, "Mr. Cryts, I'm going to hand you a newspaper and I want you to read what is outlined in yellow."

I took the paper and started reading the highlighted section. It was an article reporting that I was incarcerated in prison in Russellville, Arkansas.

When my lawyer heard that he jumped up and said, "Your Honor, I object!" Bill just had a fit about that.

The judge said, "I want the defense counsel and the prosecutor to approach the bench."

They both walked over there and started talking. Shortly after that Bill came back over to me and said, "Wayne, we are going to have this trial declared a mistrial."

I said, "What do you mean a mistrial?"

He said, "They are not allowed to bring into evidence the fact that you had been in jail previously. That will prejudice the jury, because they may assume that if you had been in jail before that you are guilty."

I said, "Bill, I'm not going to allow this to be declared a mistrial. I wanted a jury trial just like I did in the other one and I want the jury to decide if I am innocent or guilty. I want to hear their verdict."

He said, "Wayne, we have got to declare this a mistrial."

I said, "No, we don't have to declare this a mistrial."

Bill just turned around and walked back to the bench and I could hear him talking to the judge.

Then, the judge said, "I want to see the defense counsel and the prosecutor in my chambers right now!"

They started to walk off and I hollered, "Bill, come here a minute!"

He said, "What is it?"

I said, "I don't want you going in the chambers with the judge."

He said, "What do you mean, you don't want me going in the chambers?"

I said, "I don't want you going into the chambers with those guys."

He said, "Why?"

I said, "I don't trust you guys. You are getting ready to go in there and make a deal. I'm not going to allow you to go in there and do that."

He said, "Wayne I have got to. The judge has ordered me to go to the chambers with him."

I said, "Bill, you work for me and I'm paying your salary, not the judge. I'm telling you, you're not going in there."

He said, "Wayne, I have to go in there!"

I said, "Bill, you're fired!"

He said, "Wayne, you can't fire me right here in court!"

I said, "Bill, I'm telling you, I do not want you going to the chambers with the judge and prosecutor."

I just had a feeling that they had cooked up a deal between them or were about to.

Bill said, "Wayne, what am I going to tell the judge?"

I said, "Tell him that I don't trust you guys."

By now, the judge was really getting impatient. Bill walked over to the bench and told him what I had said. All of sudden, his face turned red and then the red began to move all the way to the top of his head. I thought he was going to have a stroke right there.

The judge sat there for a little bit staring at me and then said, "Mr. Cryts, I need to see the attorneys in my chambers. This court requests your presence in the chambers with them. Would that be acceptable to you?"

I said, "Yes, Your Honor. That would be fine."

I went back to the chambers with them. Then, they began putting on the biggest dog and pony show about "declaring this a mistrial."

Bill said to the prosecutor, "Now, you know that you are not supposed to do that!"

And they continued to go back and forth at each other.

Then, the judge said, "Mr. Cryts, it is my understanding that you do not want this declared a mistrial. Is that correct?"

I said, "Yes, Your Honor. That is correct."

He said, "Even though your lawyer is advising you that this may never be retried again?"

I said, "Your Honor, I want to get this behind me one way or the other. I will not accept a mistrial."

The judge said, "All right. Let's proceed."

We went back to the courtroom and continued with the trial. There was one other time that my lawyer and prosecutor got in a big hurrah. Again, the judge said, "I want to see the attorneys in my chambers. Mr. Cryts, the court requests your presence also."

We went back to the judge's chambers and they got it resolved. Then, we went back to the courtroom and continued. When all the testimony and summations were finally over, the judge indicated to the jury that this was an open and shut case. He gave the jury its instructions and sent them out to make their decision.

My family and I went out in the hall to wait for a verdict. We felt all the pressure that we had been through in previous trials as we sat there waiting for the jury to decide my fate. Once again, my life was in the jury's hands. All we could do was sit there, say some prayers, and wait. When the jury had reached a decision, my lawyer came out and got us.

When we were all seated, the judge asked, "Has the jury reached a verdict?"

The foreman stood up and said, "Yes, Your Honor, we have."

The bailiff took the paper up to the judge. He opened it up, read it, and said, "The ladies and gentlemen of the jury find the defendant not guilty."

Then, the judge began to scold the jury for finding me not guilty. He even used some vulgar language toward them. The judge went absolutely berserk. Finally, he said, "Court dismissed," and stomped out.

Everybody that was there with us was very happy and we did the hugging and kissing thing again. I thanked Bill for everything that he had done. He was shocked with the verdict himself.

We went back to the motel to relax. Everybody was so relieved to get the trial over with. The next morning, the newspaper headlines reported, "Judge Apologizes for His Conduct in Wayne Cryts Trial." The article quoted Judge Eisele's mother as saying, "I am so ashamed of the conduct of my son in the Wayne Cryts Trial." It concluded with a quote from Judge Eisele that stated, "You know, when you are against a twelve-person jury and your own mother, maybe I was wrong."

My family and I were surprised when I was sent a notice on February 17, 1983, that I had to be in court again in three weeks by the order of Judge Eisele. He had charged William Jewell, Evans Ipock, Sandy, my father, and me with "civil contempt of court."

We requested a jury trial again, but were refused. According to the judge, this was a non-jury offence. I could not believe that we were not allowed to be tried before a jury. But, my lawyer told me that the judge had a right to make that decision. Then, Bill told me that the judicial system was determined to get me one way or another. We just went through the motions of the trial knowing that we would be found guilty this time. Judge Eisele had total control over this trial.

When the trial was over, Judge Eisele found each of us guilty as we expected. But, he dismissed the charges against William, Evans, Sandy and my father. Then, he fined me $341,000 that was to be paid to the bankruptcy trustee and if at least one-third of the judgment was not paid within a year, it would be increased by $50,000. I don't know if that fine and judgment are still on the books or not, but I have never paid it.

Attempt to Confiscate Assets

When the judge realized that I would not and could not pay the fine, a court order was issued to confiscate my weapons.

A reporter from Cape Girardeau, Missouri, called me and said, "Wayne, the federal marshals have just received a court order to confiscate your weapons."

I said, "Confiscate my weapons?"

He said, "Yes, that's the way it reads. What are you going to do?"

"I guess I will turn my guns in to them if that is what I am supposed to do."

I then thanked him for the call and told him that I would call the marshal's office and find out what was going on. I called the Federal Marshals Office in Cape Girardeau, told them who I was, and asked to speak to a federal marshal.

When a marshal got on the phone, I said, "I understand that you have a court order to confiscate my weapons."

He said, "Mr. Cryts, we haven't had this court order an hour. How, in the world, did you find out about it?"

I said, "I was just informed about the court order and was calling to find out if it is true."

He said, "Yes sir, it's true. We do have a court order to confiscate your weapons. What are you going to do?"

I said, "I'm not sure just yet what I'm going to do, but I know what I'm not going to do and that's barricade myself in the house and have a shoot out with you folks!"

He laughed and told me that he was relieved to hear that. Then, I told him that Sandy and I were going to be in Cape the next day and if he would tell me how I could legally transport the guns, we would bring them up there and turn them in.

The marshal said, "You are willing to give up your guns?"

I said, "Yes, I'm willing to bring them up there and give them to you. But, I want you to tell me how I can legally transport my guns without violating some type of law."

He told me to break them down and lay them in the back seat where they could be seen.

The next morning, Sandy and I got up, put the guns in the back seat, and drove up the Federal Court Building. I walked upstairs to the Federal Marshals Office and told them I had my guns out in the car. They told me that they appreciated me bringing the guns to them, and then we walked out to the car. We packed up all the guns, carried them up to their office, and they fixed me a receipt for the guns.

Judge John Oliver set a date to advertise the sale of my guns to be held on the court house steps. However, I had to be in Washington, D.C., the day of the sale to testify on the bankruptcy legislation. I asked Sandy if she would be willing to go up and give a little talk on the court house steps asking people not to bid on the guns. Because, I had already called Bob Hardin and Bill Maddox about trying to buy the guns back for me and they had agreed to do so. I just wanted Sandy to inform everybody that the neighbors of Wayne Cryts would like to buy the guns and would really appreciate it if nobody else would bid on them. That was all she was going to say.

On the day of the sale, just before it was to begin, Sandy walked up on the court house steps and started to give her speech. But, Judge Oliver told her to get off the steps, because that wasn't any place to make a public speech. I'm glad I was in Washington, D.C., because the court house is a public place. If Sandy wanted to make a speech, she was perfectly within her rights. Luckily, most of the people there did not appreciate the judge speaking to Sandy that way, so my neighbors were able to buy the guns back for me without spending a lot of money.

Shortly after that, Judge Oliver ordered me to come to Cape Girardeau in an effort to discover what assets I had, if any. It was my understanding that it is common to take the Fifth Amendment in this situation. During this type of hearing, the judge tries to determine what assets a person has and where they are located, so that they can be confiscated.

When the day of the hearing came, I choose not to take the Fifth. Instead, I brought in fifteen boxes of letters from people all over the United States and I had mixed all the paperwork and titles to everything I owned in with those letters. When we walked in to Judge Oliver's office with all those boxes, he looked at us like we were crazy.

The judge began by asking for a particular piece of information. At that time, I would reach in one of the boxes, take out a letter, and read it. Then, I would say, "No, that's not it," and I would put that letter down, pick up another one, and read it. This went on for two or three hours.

Finally, the judge said, "It's time to take a lunch break."

When he said that, I took all those letters that I had just read and put them back in the box.

After the lunch break, we all met back in his office and he began by asking me another question about my assets. So, I reached in the same box and started going through it again.

Judge Oliver said, "Mr. Cryts, you have already gone through that box."

I said, "I'm sorry judge, I put everything back in there just before we left for lunch and now it's all mixed up again. I don't know if I have looked at this one or not."

This went on for a couple more hours.

Finally, he said, "I'm kind of at a dilemma as to what to do. This is very unusual. Most people take the Fifth Amendment. I didn't anticipate you bringing all this stuff up here. It's doubtful that you are ever going to find anything that I'm looking for in all those boxes."

He stopped us there, we loaded up our boxes, and went back home. I never received another notice about that again.

National Media Speaking Requests

I began to have people calling from all over the country wanting me to speak to them, because of all the publicity that I had received over the past couple of years. Talk shows, radio programs, magazine and newspaper reporters all called, asking me to appear on their show and give them interviews.

Sandy got to where she hated to answer the phone. She is a quiet person and enjoys "the simple life." She just took things one day at time. I remember a song by Christy Lane "One Day at a Time" that she said helped her so much. Sandy talked to the people who called and took messages for me, so I could call them back. Every once in a while, Sandy would call her sister and ask her to come over and answer the phone calls for a couple of days so that she could get some rest.

While I was out on the road doing the interviews, George and Mona Foster would call Sandy every other day to check on her and the kids. They lived close to us at the time and were very helpful. We cannot say enough good things about our friends and neighbors.

I appeared on The *Phil Donahue Show*, *The Sandy Freeman Report*, *The 700 Club* twice, The Derry Brownfield Report, and several others. I was interviewed by reporters from the *Wall Street Journal, People, Times, Newsweek,* the *Saturday Evening Post,* and many local TV, radio programs, and newspapers.

The one show that stands out the most in my mind was *The David Susskind Show* out of New York. David Susskind was a talk show host and moderator for twenty-nine years. At that time, it was the longest running talk show in the United States. It was syndicated in most of the larger cities.

David Susskind had had many well known featured guests including Harry S. Truman, Richard M. Nixon, Robert F. Kennedy, and Nikita Khrushchev. But, I was the first farmer that he had ever had on his show.

I remember that I had come in from doing some work on the farm one day and Sandy told me about a phone call that she had received.

Sandy said she answered the phone and it was Jean Kennedy, a producer for *The David Susskind Show.*

Jean introduced herself and asked Sandy, "Can I speak to Wayne Cryts?"

Sandy told her, "Wayne's out on a tractor working."

Jean Kennedy replied, "Wayne drives a tractor?"

"Yes, he does."

"What time does he usually get in?"

"He usually gets home around 7:00 this time of the year."

"We would like for Wayne to come to New York and appear on our program. Would it be all right if I called him at that time?"

"Sure."

A little after 7:00 that evening, the phone rang and I answered it. The lady said, "Is this Mr. Cryts?"

I said, "Yes, this is Wayne."

She said, "This is Jean Kennedy. I talked to your wife earlier today and I produce *The David Susskind Show*. We have been hearing a lot about agriculture and the elevator issue that you have been involved with in the news lately. I am calling to see if you would be willing to come to New York and appear on our show."

I said, "Yes, I would be glad to."

She said, "Mr. Cryts, I will make all the arrangements and will get back to you."

I said, "That will be fine."

A couple of days later, she called me back and told me that she had made arrangements for me to come to New York. Then, she said, "Mr. Cryts you will fly out of St. Louis into LaGuardia. When the plane lands, you will simply follow the people off the plane to the first exit that you come to, then go out that exit, and there will be a line of taxicabs sitting out there. Go to the first cab, get in, and give them the address to our studio. The cab driver will bring you to our front door. Go in, tell them who you are, and that you need to see Jean Kennedy. You understand that you will fly to LaGuardia, follow the people off of the plane, go to the first exit, go outside, get in a cab, give them our address, and the cab driver will take you to our front door."

I said, "Jean, I think I can do that." I think she must have thought that I was some poor uneducated farmer that had never been out of Stoddard County.

When I told some of my friends about our conversation, it became a joke around my area. People would come up to me and ask how to get to *The David Susskind Show*. I would tell them: "I fly to La Guardia, follow the people off the plane, go to the first exit, get in the cab, give the driver the address, get dropped off at their front door, and walk in." Then, we would burst out laughing.

Anyway, I made my journey to the big city and managed to get to the studio without any problems. I walked in and Jean met me at the desk. Of course, I had on my cowboy boots, denim jeans and jacket, and my AAM hat. That was the kind of clothes that I wore nearly everyday. I looked like a farmer and was proud of it. We talked a little bit, she told me about David Susskind, and the show.

Then, Jean said, "Before you appear on the show, we need to take you to our make-up artist and he'll fix you up."

I said, "All right."

She had someone take me to the make-up room. I went in and sat down in a chair with a big mirror and lights in front of it. Pretty soon, this guy came in. He had on fancy cloths, his hair was slicked back, and he had on patent leather shoes. Upon entering the room, he stopped immediately, looked at me, then walked over to the chair and turned it around.

He stepped back and said, "Mr. Cryts, I'm here to do the make-up for you before you go on *The David Susskind Show.*"

I said, "All right, Jean Kennedy told me that someone would be in to put some make-up on me."

He said, "Mr. Cryts could you remove your cap for me please?"

"No, I'm going to wear my cap."

"You are going to wear you cap on *The David Susskind Show?*"

"Yes sir."

"I have never put make-up on anybody with a cap on before."

"I've never been made up before, so this is going to be a new experience for both of us."

He stepped over to the make-up table and started to work. He used powder, rouge, and even put color on my lips. He worked and worked until he finally figured that was all he could do with this face.

When he was finished, I walked out to the stage and Mr. Susskind was standing there. You talk about a "scholarly looking gentleman": he had on a pin striped suit, his silver hair was combed just right, and he very graciously shook hands with me. We sat down and chatted for quite a little bit before the show started.

When it started, Mr. Susskind said, "Mr. Cryts, I've never had a farmer on the show before."

Then, he started asking me some very good questions that were direct and to the point. I was impressed with him and felt good about our conversation. And I remember somewhere in the show, he said, "Mr. Cryts, after listening to you, I've got to believe that Paul Revere must be your greatest hero."

I paused a little bit and said, "Mr. Susskind, no, that's not true. I'm sure Paul Revere was a great man. But, when Paul Revere was riding through the streets of Boston shouting 'The British are coming,' for all I know he was just getting the hell out of town. My heroes are the people who were lying in bed asleep that heard the warning and were willing to get up, get dressed, and go fight the battles. Those people were my heroes! There are all kinds of Paul Reveres riding through the country shouting about the problems and warning us about apparent dangers. But, what this country needs are more American people who are willing to stand up and get involved, take care of the battles, and win the war."

I could just see the expression on his face change when I said that and could tell that I had really gotten to him. We seemed to connect with each other from that point forward. The show was simply a question and answer session and the longer we talked, the more he wanted to know.

Mr. Susskind said, "You know, it really makes sense to me, that we should allow the American farmer to make a fair profit. They are the backbone of our society."

He was astonished at the farmers standing together and how they won the battle to remove the grain at the elevator. To me, that was probably one of the best talk shows that I had ever been on.

The *60 Minutes Show* that airs on CBS had rooms reserved at the Ramada Inn in Sikeston for the weekend before the day that we went in to remove my grain. They had told me that they wanted to be here to film the entire event from the time I was to go in and get the beans until I had removed them for the Ristine property. But, they never showed up.

Harry Thomason of Columbia Pictures called after we had removed the beans and wanted to do a movie about what had happened. His wife, Linda Bloodworth, who was originally from Poplar Bluff, Missouri, and he had been following the story from the beginning. Mr. Thomason actually flew in from California to meet with me at the Ramada Inn at Sikeston and told me that he wanted to make a movie about this and would not take no for an answer. I told him that I was not interested in doing a movie, because I was not doing this to capitalize on the situation. Instead, I was fighting for a cause. That was hard for him to understand. Harry called constantly until I agreed to a deal with them. He told me that a contract would be in the mail the next day and they wanted it back as soon as possible. But, the contract never came and I never heard anything else from him after that.

In fact, Mr. Thomason was not the only movie producer that called. We had several calls for a few weeks after we removed our grain from the Ristine Elevator.

Then, they all stopped as quickly as they started and we did not get one more call about a movie after that.

I have always wondered why the *60 Minutes* people never showed up and the motion picture people stopped calling.

One Man Can Make a Difference

I was taught as a young boy to work hard, respect my elders, and obey the law. But, I have found that, sometimes, laws are not always right. I was taught in school about an event that happened back in 1776 called the American Revolution where a group of farmers and businessmen had the courage to stand up against the mighty King of England and won.

I started this whole thing, because a judge ordered my grain to be sold as part of the assets of the owners of the Ristine Elevator who filed bankruptcy. I had warehouse receipts for every bushel of grain that I had in the elevator. I was merely renting storage space for my private property until I decided to sell it.

I did not plan for any of this to happen, but I could not stand by and watch the grain that my family had worked hard through the long, hot summer to grow and harvest be sold to help make the trustee and other lawyers wealthy.

My family and I had decided that we would sacrifice everything we had and even go to jail to protect our private property. From the very beginning, I planned to do this in a peaceful manner, with no violence or physical harm to anyone. The best weapon that I had was a smiling face, the willingness to shake hands, and talk with anyone and everyone, whether they were friend or foe. I always tried to inform the law enforcement officials and news media about every move that I made prior to it happening, so there would be no surprises.

I believe that justice and freedom does not depend so much upon a person's willingness to stand up and fight for it himself as much as it does that person's willingness to stand up and fight for others. If our family had to stand alone at the Ristine Elevator, we would have lost our fight. But, people from all over the nation came to our aid, like knights in shining armor to stand by our side.

Thomas Jefferson once said on January 30, 1787, "I hold it that a little rebellion, now and then, is a good thing, and as necessary in the political world as storms are in the physical."

WE WON!

Abraham Lincoln, in a speech in Cincinnati, Ohio, on September 15, 1859, said, "The people of the United States are the rightful matters of both congress and the courts, not to overthrow the constitution, but to overthrow the men who pervert the constitution."

Thomas Jefferson, in reference to the Supreme Court said, "This member of the government was at first considered the most harmless and helpless of all its organs. But, it has proved that the power of declaring what law is, *ad libitum*, by sapping and mining slyly and without alarm the foundations of the Constitution, can do what open force would not dare to attempt."

I truly believe that Judge Baker had a personal vendetta against me and did his best to put me behind bars. Ultimately, Judge Baker resigned from the bench as a Federal Bankruptcy Judge. We considered that a major victory for us.

I was able to testify in Washington, D.C., thanks to Senators Dole and Grassley, about the dire need to change the Federal Bankruptcy Law. I believe that the law had to be changed to provide protection for the American farmer who worked hard to plant, grow, and harvest his crop. I continued to fight for the changes in the Federal Bankruptcy Law until those changes happened.

By testifying before a variety of states' congressional committees, I also helped farmers in many states across the nation fight to get bankruptcy laws in their states revised to help them. The State of Illinois developed the best revision to help protect their farmers. It was a good, simple law that worked for everyone. In most states, elevator owners are required to buy a bond, but that bond usually doesn't cover but ten percent of the grain that is stored there. The State of Illinois set up a fund in which the elevator owners would pay the exact same amount that they would have paid for the bond into that fund. The elevator owners and farmers both liked it. The elevator owners did not pay anymore than they normally did and the farmers had one hundred percent protection on their grain. If an elevator owner would go bankrupt, money would be taken out of that fund, and the farmers would be paid what the market price was the day the elevator declared bankruptcy. Then, a check would be sent to the farmers within one hundred-twenty days. The fund would continue to grow each year as the elevator owners paid their fees to the state. If there were losses larger than the fund had in it, the state agreed to guarantee this fund with general revenue money. The legislature had set a minimum ceiling for the fund. When the account exceeded that level, then the State of Illinois took their money back out of that fund. Another reason the elevator owners liked this plan was that once the fund had reached the ceiling, then they could stop paying their fees. In addition, they did not have to pay again unless there were losses that lowered the revenue in the fund below the minimum ceiling.

I had hoped that we could get all the states to adopt a law similar to the one Illinois had. It was a very good plan that worked for the farmer and the elevator owners. I had also hoped to get national bankruptcy legislation reformed to match theirs as well.

The AAM and I continued to work for about three years before we finally got legislation passed at the national level on elevator owner bankruptcies. I was fighting for this all along and thought it was a good victory. Hundreds of people testified before congress and worked hard to get the law changed.

Over 140 grain elevators in 22 states had gone bankrupt from 1974 to 1982. These bankruptcies tied up over a billion dollars worth of grain that belonged to farmers all over the nation. After a bankruptcy was over and all the legal fees and court costs were paid, the poor farmer would receive as little as five percent for every dollar's worth of grain that he had stored up to fifty-nine percent. The grain was one hundred percent theirs, so why did they not deserve to be paid one hundred percent of their money? After all, they are the ones that toiled over their crops from the day it was planted until the day it was harvested.

I have had numerous farmers call me since that time to let me know that their elevator had gone bankrupt. And to tell me that because of changes made to the bankruptcy laws, they were able to get paid for their grain.

I was a part of the American Agriculture Movement for several years and was eventually elected as vice-president of the national organization. I was asked several times to be the president of this great organization, but declined so I could devote more of my time helping farmers save their farms in times of economic hardship. I attended some of the Farm Aid concerts that Willie Nelson and John Cougar Melancamp put on. I also became very good friends with Eddie Albert who was most notably known for his role on the TV sitcom *Green Acres*. Eddie became actively involved in our effort to help save the family farms across the nation. We remained close friends until his death.

I am currently working on my second book about my involvement in the American Agriculture Movement organization. I joined the AAM in 1977 and was part of the tractorcades that converged on Washington, D.C., and the Chicago Board of Trade to help bring attention to the plight of the American farmer. There are several references to the AAM throughout the book. When I decided to remove my grain from the elevator, the farmers in that organization rallied around me in support of my family farm and protection of my personal property.

I want to end this book by saying I could not have made it through the trials and tribulations without the love, strength, and support of my family, friends, farmers, and plain folk from across this mighty nation. Finally, I thank God above that I live in a country as fine as the good ol' USA.

Your Support Is My Strength

Wayne and his family could not have removed their beans from the elevator storage facilities on three different occasions, fought through the many court battles without the support of their friends, neighbors, and people from across the nation.

Wayne did his best to remember the names of those that helped him, but after twenty-five years, it was difficult to recall the names of every person that helped in some way. Therefore, some names may have been unintentionally left out.

Wayne wanted to finish this book by saying, "To those of you who are listed below and anyone else that may have been forgotten, I would like to express my deepest appreciation. Your strength was my support."

Adkins, Ruben

Alexander, Bill Representative

Allen, Wayne

Armstrong, Dean

Armstrong, Lola

Ashcroft, John

Astin, Randall

Bader, Frank

Bailey, F. Lee

Battles, Terry

Beasley, Ken

Beck, Joe

Beck, Joe Jr.

Beeson, Cecil

Bell, Richard

Bitner, Lynn

Blair, Bob

Blankenship, Brad

Block, John R.

Bolin, James Sheriff

Broughton, Joe

Brown, Bob

Brown, Calvin

Brown, Cary

Brown, Fred

Brown, Pauline

Buck, Bill

Buck, Kent

Burgess, Danny

Burns, Ludis

Buschman, Helen (Page)

Calse, Ken

Campbell, Buel

Campbell, Herman

Carpenter, Ernest

Carter, Paul

Chapman, Odis

Cherry, Mel

Chestnut, Perry

Childers, Tim

Clark, Claude

Clinton, Bill

Cookson, Gail

Cooper, Charlie

Cothran, Jack

Cowan, Lynn

Cox, Leonard

Crego, Ken

Cryts, Crystal

Cryts, Monte

Cryts, Paula

Cryts, Terry

Cryts, Tyler

Curl, Tom

Daniels, Robert

Deal, Edie

Deardorff, Gary

Deardorff, Jesse L.

DeBore, Bonnie

DeBore, Stan

Deichman, Don

DeLay, Beatrice

DeLay, Ralph

Dole, Bob Senator

Droke, Pete

Dumey, Dan

Eagleton, Tom Senator

Eck, Pearl

Eck, Robert

Ellsworth, Sam

Emerson, Bill Congressman

Essary, Tom

Estes, Mike

Evans, Homer

Faries, Alvin

Faries, Bill

Farney, Ben

Faubus, Orval E.Governor

Ford, Jerry

Foster, George

Foster, Harlan

Fowler, Gary

Fowler, Roy

Freeman, Bob

Kimble, Don

Kirby, Darrell

Knapp, Lyman Mr. & Mrs.

Kneibert, Dick

Koster, Donald

Laffoon, W.H.

Lane, James

Lane, Sonny

Lane, Vic

Lasiter, Robert

Lassiter, Jack

LaValles, Charles E. Jr.

Lewis, Carrie

Lewis, Jack

Linville, Herman

Long, James

Lowe, Dean

Lowery, Norma

Maddox, Bill

Martin, Sonny

Matlack, Bill

Mattlack, Larry

McAlister, Bobbie

McAnally, Sam

McCann, H.C.

McGhee, Robert

McPherson, Henry

Meek, Marvin

Menees, Roger

Metlock, Willier L.

Minus, Roger

Moore, Glenn

Moore, Kenny

Moore, Tressa

Morgan, Marvin

Mouser, Ralph Sheriff

Murphy, Borden

Murphy, Quincy

Nellis, Alden

Newcomb, Doyle

Nowell, N.J.

Nowell, Rich

Ochoa, Gregg

Ochs, Darrell

Oerke, Marvin

Oliveaux, Jim

Palmer, Larry

Pankhursd, Cecil

Parr, P.L.

Patterson, Larry

Peterson, Wayne

Pierce, Kay

Pigg, Jack

Pipkin, Waldo

Placzek, Kevin

Porche, Johnny

Priddle, Harlan

Pryor, David Senator

Puckett, Peter

Putz, Donald J.

Putz, Lee E.

Radcliff, Orlie

Ragsdale, Larry

Raulston, Russell

Reagan, Ronald President

Reno, Merle

Richardson, T-Bone

Riddle, Ted

Riley, Edwin

Riley, Robert Jr.

Riney, Bud

Rink, Paul

Roberts, Pat Congressman

Robertson, Ricky

Rogers, Neal

Rogers, Ralph

Runyan, Jack

Russell, Ron Mayor

Sadler, Jerry

Sanner, Harvey Joe

Schaper, Keith

Schluter, Dale

Schluterman, Al

Schluterman, Ben R.

Schluterman, Marty

Schollenberger, Charles

Schott, Carl

Schroder, Gene

Scott, Hobart

Scott, Steve

Seltman, Jeff

Sentell, Chester

Sentell, Danny

Sentell, Harley

Sentell, James

Senter, David

Shrum, Ron

Sifford, Bill

Sifford, Eddie

Sifford, Frank

Sifford, Marty

Slavens, George

Smith, Joe

Stanton, Fred

Steward, James

Stewart, Charlie

Stewart, Gary

Stewart, Sammy

Stobaugh, W.A.

Stockton, H. M.

Stoner, Bob

Stoops, Barb

Stoops, Ed

Stride, Harold

Stride, Ruth

Stuart, Bob

Sweet, Terry

Taylor, Bayless

Taylor, Ferral

Taylor, Mary

Taylor, Terry

Temples, Alvin

Temples, Bud

Tetley, Bob

Thompson, Eric

Thornton, Bob

Tillman, Roy Jr.

Tillmon, Lawrence

Tinnin, Nelson B. Senator

Tucker, Gary

Tucker, J. D.

Tucker, Jack

Tucker, Larry

Turner, Tom

Vancil, Kenny

Wade, Jeff

Walker, Greg

Wamble, Pat

Ward, Adrian

Warden, Jerry

Webb, Arlene

Webb, Walter

Welty, Carlos

Welty, Wanda

Willis, Tommy

Withrow, Jim

Woolard, Gilbert

Zych, Tim

About the Author

Air Force veteran **Jerry Hobbs** was raised in Thayer, Missouri, located in the foothills of the Ozarks. He earned his BSE and MSE degrees from Arkansas State University and completed his specialist degree in education administration at Southwest Missouri State University.

978-0-595-37668-1
0-595-37668-1

Printed in the United States
42647LVS00007B/1-186